"Then **Junior** said to **Jeff**..."

The Best NASCAR Stories Ever Told

by David Poole

and

Jim McLaurin

TRIUMPH
B O O K S
CHICAGO

Library of Congress Cataloging-in-Publication Data

Poole, David, 1959–
Then junior said to Jeff—: the best NASCAR stories ever told / by David Poole and James McLaurin.
    p. cm.
Includes bibliographical references.
ISBN-13: 978-1-57243-847-7
ISBN-10: 1-57243-847-9
1. Stock car racing—United States—Miscellanea. 2. Automobile racing drivers—United States—Conduct of life. 3. NASCAR (Association) I. McLaurin, James, 1946– II. Title.
GV1029.9.S74P65 2006
796.72—dc22
                                                    2005032835

This book is available in quantity at special discounts for your group or organization. For further information, contact:

Triumph Books
542 South Dearborn Street
Suite 750
Chicago, Illinois 60605
(312) 939-3330
Fax (312) 663-3557

Printed in U.S.A.
ISBN-13: 978-1-57243-847-7
ISBN-10: 1-57243-847-9
Design by Patricia Frey
Photos courtesy of AP/Wide World Photos

For Leonard Poole, for whom hard work was the story of his life.
—David Poole

For my wife, Inez. Anything short of another War and Peace *fails to do her justice, but for now this'll have to do.*
—Jim McLaurin

table of
contents

foreword

Nothing is quite as bad as a rainy day at a race track.

Race cars, at least NASCAR's stock cars, run on slick tires—tires with no treads—so they can't run on a wet track. Or even a damp one. So when it rains at a race track, there's nothing going on.

But in some ways, there's no place better to be than a track on a rainy day. Especially if you wander into the right truck or walk up under the right canopy or shed, where people are gathered to take refuge from the elements.

Sometimes, when you're just trying not to get soaked, you wind up standing around a crowd of guys who've been coming to the track all of their lives. They haven't read about NASCAR's history; they've lived it.

One of the best things about NASCAR is that the sport hasn't yet been around so long that all of the people who've been there from the very beginning are gone. Some of them are still with us, and boy, do they have stories to tell.

Once in while, you'll see Richard Petty and David Pearson in the same room. Once in a while, you'll catch a man like Lowe's Motor Speedway president H. A. "Humpy" Wheeler in the right mood, and he'll get that faraway look in his eyes. He'll be back somewhere in the 1950s, remember something he saw or heard, and he'll take you back there with him.

It's great, too, that so many of the guys who've lived NASCAR history are so willing to share it. Try to stop Buddy Baker from telling you stories. Go ahead, give it a shot.

This book is just a sampler of some of the stories that Jim McLaurin and I have heard and passed along during our careers covering stock-car racing. There are so many good ones that it's actually a lot harder than it'd seem to be to sit down and recall them when you need to, but it sure was fun trying.

Jim—nobody in racing knows him by any name other than Jimmy Mac—covered racing for *The State* newspaper in Columbia, South Carolina, for longer than he cares to talk about. He knows where too many of the great places to go are (that aren't the race track) in places like Darlington and Daytona.

Throughout this book, when you see the initials J.M. behind a story, that means it's one Jimmy Mac is telling you. Sometimes you'll see a notation following his initials. Because we made Jimmy Mac tell most of the stories from more than just the past few years, and because we wanted to make sure the stories we were telling had as many of the particulars right as we could, he checked with some sources and has cited them out of fairness to those.

The stories with D.P. after them are mine. They're stories I've heard and/or written about since I started covering the Cup Series full-time in 1997 for the *Charlotte* (North Carolina) *Observer*, which has been covering stock-car racing as extensively as any newspaper in the country for more than 40 years.

Between us, what we've tried to do is brush across nearly 60 years of heroics and hijinks, picking out just a few of the memorable moments that make covering this sport such an often entertaining and always interesting job.

Enjoy the ride.

—David Poole
November 2005

chapter 1
In the Beginning…

*Bill Rexford, 1950
NASCAR Winston Cup
Champion, at practice
run, 3-29-51*

In the sport's earliest days, "organized racing" was almost an oxymoron.

School of Hard Knocks

In racing's formative years, some race promoters were notorious for taking off with the gate receipts before the race, leaving the drivers—whether they liked it or not—to race just for fun.

The drivers themselves were an unruly lot, often making up the rules—and the tracks—as they went. Safety equipment, what there was of it, was rudimentary at best, and more often than not, non-existent.

Long-time racing official Ernie Moore once described a race somewhere in southern Georgia in which "one old boy knocked himself . . . about five times." The race was a 15-lap feature run in a recently harvested cornfield. The "track" quickly deteriorated, Moore said, particularly in one corner.

"There was a hole about 5' deep," he remembered. "The cars would hit that hole and the driver's head would bang against the roof of the car. They'd hang out of those cars when they hit that hole. That one old boy knocked himself cuckoo about five times, and every time, he'd crash into another car."

That day, Moore said, the fans saved that driver from himself: "Some of the spectators would pour water on him, and he'd take off again. "The fifth time he did it, they didn't bother waking him up." —J.M. (Hunter, pp. 16)

Feels Like the First Time

The first race in what is now known as the NASCAR Nextel Cup Series took place on June 19, 1949, on a three-quarter—mile dirt track in Charlotte, North Carolina.

The track is no longer there—now it's just a field between two highways near the city's airport. But on that afternoon, a 150-mile race on a rutted track that took its toll on man and machine gave birth to what is now America's premiere motorsports series.

The idea was to have cars come straight to the race track from off the showroom floor. The name of the series outlined the rulebook—it was NASCAR's new "strictly stock" series that had its first official race scheduled for that day.

The drivers were allowed to make only the most minor adjustments—removing wheel covers and adding seat belts, things like that. Many drivers went to military surplus stores and got belts to tie themselves in, while others simply used, well, belts, the ones they used to hold their pants up.

There were 33 cars entered. One was driven by a young man from Denton, North Carolina, named Archie Smith.

"It cost $25 to enter," Smith recalls. "Nobody had that. I was working for 75¢ an hour and my daddy didn't want me to go. But he finally agreed to loan me the money."

Smith had heard about the race in a radio advertisement. Jim Roper, who was from Kansas, had read about it in a comic strip in his local newspaper and made the long drive. That would turn out to be a good decision.

Smith brought his personal car down to Charlotte, taped up the headlights, buckled the doors closed with a leather belt, and strapped himself in with an old horse harness he bought at a hardware store.

But first, he made a little side trip.

"I wanted to be smarter than anybody else," Smith says. "We went to the airport and filled up with airplane gas. They came out and caught us and wanted to know what we were doing. We told them we were buying gas for the race. They were about to make us pump it all out."

But just before the race started, Smith's car would not start. He had a buddy, who was helping him in the pits, paged over the public address system. The friend brought an air tank and he and Smith blew out the gas lines and started the race.

Drivers weren't the only ones who'd heard about the race, of course. A boy living just across the Catawba River in the town of Belmont knew there was a race that day, so he walked from Belmont Abbey College, where his father was the athletics director, down to the intersection of US 74 and hitchhiked his way to the show. The young man, Howard Wheeler, later picked up the same nickname his father had: Humpy.

Archie Smith wasn't the only North Carolina driver to come to the state's largest city to race that day, either. Lee Petty drove down from Level Cross with two carloads of family and friends.

One of the cars was the one Lee raced in the event. During the race, he hooked a tire in one of the ruts the heavy cars had worn into the track's surface and flipped it. Not only did that end Petty's race, it also rendered one of the cars the Petty clan had used to get to Charlotte unworthy of making the trip back home. So after the race, the womenfolk took the working car home. Lee stayed back in Charlotte to get the other car fixed. And his young son, Richard, hitchhiked home.

When the checkered flag flew after 200 laps, Glenn Dunnaway from nearby Gastonia was the winner.

Or was he?

The springs in the 1947 Ford that Dunnaway drove had been altered. And since this was a strictly stock race, that was illegal.

So Roper, the Kansan who'd literally seen it in the funny papers, was declared the winner. —D.P.

Racing Like a Lady

To the everlasting delight of the automobile racing crowd, Louise Smith talked as good a game as she played.

"You had to fight all the time," Smith once said. "I thought men weren't supposed to hit women and women weren't supposed to hit men, but I found out it went both ways. If you won a race, you just about had to fight."

A Greenville, South Carolina, native, Smith was born in 1916 and was one of the true pioneers in racing. She was a racer before there was a NASCAR, winning 38 races in the modified division in the 1940s and '50s.

She managed to catch the eye of a young promoter named Bill France and, when she finished third in her first race at Greenville-Pickens Speedway, she and France figured they had a good thing.

"Coming in third made a lot of them mad," she said. "I think a lot of them are mad at me now. . . . But Bill France and I became good friends, and he let me race. I think I turned out to be a pretty good driver."

Racing was a novelty in itself in the early days, and Smith's presence in a male-dominated sport may have been looked at as a gimmick. But her opponents came to know her as a hard-knocking competitor who gave as good as she took.

"I let them push me around to start with," she said, "but Buddy Shuman...we were in Asheville and all out at a party one night—a big racing shebang with them and their wives—and he came up and told me he wanted to take me out to the speedway the next morning and show me something.

"He took me out to Weaverville Speedway and showed me how to bump them on the back fender and make them flip [spin out]. We practiced that thing all day Saturday, and I got to where I could do it pretty good.

"He got killed that night, but I got to where they called me 'Little Buddy Shuman' after that. I didn't have to hit but two guys who were hitting on me. I cut them a flip, and nobody didn't bother me no more."

In 1999 Smith was voted into the International Motorsports Hall of Fame at Talladega, Alabama. As of 2005, she was still one of only two women (drag racing legend Shirley Muldowney being the other) in the Hall.

She was as tough a competitor as there was in racing's wild and wooly days, gender be damned.

"They were all rough," she said. "I don't know who was the roughest. We were all friends, but once you hit that race track, you ain't got no friends.

"It's every man for hisself. And on my part, it was every woman for hisself." —J.M.

X Marks the Spot

Francis Eduardo Menendez, better known as Frank Mundy because his buddies in his hometown of Atlanta found that easier to pronounce than the former, made a couple of marks in NASCAR in its formative years.

But he was better known as a stunt car driver. Mundy spent seven years with Lucky Teter's Hell Drivers and became an expert at somersaulting a car, jumping it 120', and crashing it head-on. Especially crashing it head-on.

"I volunteered for the head-on crash because it paid $10 more a week," Mundy said. "The secret to a perfect head-on was to be able to drive the car from the back seat. You ducked behind a mattress just before impact."

Mundy won three races on NASCAR's Grand National Circuit, and he even won the pole for the second Southern 500 at Darlington—in a Studebaker—in 1951.

But he cut his racing teeth at the old Lakewood Speedway in Atlanta in the pre–World War II era. "I was knocked cold only once on a track, and it came in those early days at Lakewood," he said.

Lakewood was a dirt oval with a lake in the infield, and one of the dustier tracks around.

"The stockers kicked up so much dust you couldn't see the other cars," Mundy said. "Anytime you drive blind, you drive scared. I was judging the turns on the backstretch by a bunch of trees. When I saw them, I'd count to five or six and then straighten the car. I was busy counting when I plowed into six other cars who must have been counting, too.

"I woke up in the ambulance. After they found no broken bones, I raced back, borrowed a car, and finished second in the feature."

Mundy was one of the few drivers of that era who flew to races and let whoever he was driving for haul the car to the track. That semi-backfired on him in 1956, when he arrived at a track near Los Angeles to find his car hadn't made it.

He rented a car, painted an X on the door, and finished eighth in the race without a pit crew, extra tires, or gas. He won $100, and the car rental only came to $37, so Mundy still came out ahead. —J.M. (Cutter, pp. 432–33)

Long Time Running

Dick Rathmann's win in a 250-lap race at California's Oakland Speedway in 1954 was the first last-place-to-first-place victory in NASCAR history, but that's not the half of it.

Rathmann's journey to the checkered flag was more like a marathon than a 125-mile sprint.

Rathmann, a Californian who had come east to race stock cars, and his mechanic Jim Ellis picked up a brand new Hudson Hornet race car in Atlanta, Georgia, four days before the race to haul it out to California. The pair took turns sleeping while the other one drove, at one point motoring through a snowstorm, until they were about one hundred miles from Oakland.

Then the car they were using to tow the race car broke down. Rathmann decided to use the race car to tow the tow car to the track, and he and Ellis arrived at 1:00 AM on the day of the race. They spent the morning getting the race car in shape for qualifying and then, during his qualifying lap, the gas tank fell off, evidently having been weakened by towing the tow car, and it was unlikely that they would find a replacement.

However, another Hudson just like Rathmann's crashed during qualifying and destroyed everything on the car *but* the gas tank. Rathmann borrowed the tank and made it into the field, taking the 26th (and last) qualifying spot.

By then, the crowd had gotten wind of his extraordinary efforts in just getting to the race, and they cheered wildly as he took the lead on lap 143 and led the rest of the way.

After the race, someone pointed out to Rathmann that it had taken him less than 2½ hours (2 hours, 27 minutes, and 57 seconds) to finish the race.

A weary Rathmann smiled and said it felt more like a week. —J.M. (Engel, pp. 106)

chapter 2
Curtis and Smokey and Harry and 'Em

*Curtis Turner in 1966
Chevy (13) runs off track
at Daytona on 2-26-67*

NASCAR history is replete with colorful characters, men who've made their mark on the sport in many ways.

Well Suited to the Task

Curtis Turner made and lost several fortunes in the timber business, and no doubt could have won more NASCAR races if he'd approached racing differently. But it was said that if Turner did lose a race, he never lost a party.

Turner's parties were legendary affairs that sometimes lasted for days, and when one was over, his favorite phrase was, "There's another party startin' in 15 minutes."

On the race track, Turner's philosophy was that if it took beating and banging to get to the front—indeed, he once won a race in Asheville, North Carolina, when his was the only car left running at the end—then all the better.

The venue changes occasionally, as does the color of the suit, but Turner once drove a race in a three-piece business suit— the result of having shown up late for a race with a crushing hangover.

Or, depending on who was telling the story, about half-smashed.

"I was about half-tuned when I got to the race and didn't even have time to change my clothes," Turner himself said. "So I just got in the car with my suit and tie on and took off runnin'. Blew a tire and finished fourth.

"I told my sponsors they ought to want their drivers to dress like gentlemen." —J.M. (Chapin, pp. 41)

The Honor System?

Country and western star Marty Robbins loved racing as much as he did singing, often leaving the Grand Ole Opry show as soon as his number was over to go out to the speedway in Nashville to beat and bang with the locals.

If he didn't have an engagement, he sometimes followed the show on the road.

Racing was his hobby. And while he didn't have the money it took to run up front, he enjoyed racing back in the pack with the rest of the "independents."

Well, except maybe once.

In 1972 at Talladega Superspeedway, Robbins surprised even himself by going a lot faster than he'd ever gone, certainly faster than NASCAR had expected him to. Late in the race, he was clocked at 188 mph, when he had only qualified at 177. He finished 18th in the race.

Even he suspected something fishy, so he asked NASCAR technical inspector Bill Gazaway to have a look at his carburetor. Someone had given him one that was a trifle larger than it should have been.

Robbins refused the $250 bonus for being the highest-finishing rookie in the race, and NASCAR disqualified him for the illegal carburetor. The incident cost him more than $1,000.

Robbins didn't care, saying that it was worth it just to see the look on Joe Frasson's face when he blew by. —J.M.

Just a Guy Doing His Job

Sam McQuagg, who raced on NASCAR's Grand National Circuit in the 1960s, might be best remembered as the other guy in the photo when Cale Yarborough jumped the fence at Darlington in 1965.

But McQuagg did have his one day in the sun.

McQuagg, in fact, was more remarkable by the fact that there was little remarkable about him in an era when bigger-than-life heroes such as Yarborough, David Pearson, and Richard Petty ruled racing.

McQuagg was the son of a carpenter from Columbus, Georgia, and was a man of simple pleasures. Devoted to his wife, McQuagg did not race on Friday nights because that's when he took her out to dinner. Once, when asked why he would not attend a racing dinner on Sunday evening, he said, "My favorite TV program, *Bonanza*, is on, and I wouldn't miss it for the world."

In 1965 McQuagg won rookie of the year honors for five top 10 finishes in 15 races, and the Chrysler camp steered him into a highly regarded Ray Nichels Dodge for the next season. When the circuit got to Daytona, Florida, in July for the Firecracker 400, he put it all together.

He charged into the lead for the first nine laps, then settled in until it was time to race. He battled Jim Paschal, Buddy Baker, and even the legendary Curtis Turner until taking the lead for good for the final 30 laps.

It turned out to be the only major league win of his career, but he celebrated in typical McQuagg fashion: he took his wife out to a nice steak house in Daytona, then drove all the way back to Columbus.

The next morning he was out at dawn, delivering papers for a neighborhood boy who was sick. Maybe in part because the banner headline in his hometown paper read: McQuagg Wins at Daytona.

"It was great for my garage business," he said. —J.M.

"Hey, Look Where You're Walking"

Cale Yarborough was still a kid the first time he raced at
Daytona, in a modified race, but he found out that he had
arrived. Not because he'd led the race, but because he was
invited to Robinson's, a bar on South Atlantic Avenue where all
the hotshot racers hung out.

Curtis Turner and Joe Weatherly, two of wildest party men in
racing, frequented the place because their "party pad" was right
across the street.

About midway through his first evening at Robinson's,
Yarborough said he was approached by a well-tuned Turner,
who invited him to stop by anytime. Yarborough was impressed,
but he didn't know quite what to make of the invitation. He
noted that the "pad" was more than a little rundown and wondered aloud why two such big-time drivers as Turner and
Weatherly would stay in such a shabby hostelry when they could
have afforded any place on the beach.

"Well, kid," Turner told him, "when I get ready to go home at
night, I figure the worst thing that can happen to me is someone
might step on my fingers." —J.M. (Yarborough, Neely, pp. 139)

The Best Damn Storyteller in Town

Henry "Smokey" Yunick was the most innovative auto mechanic
racing has ever seen, and maybe the best storyteller of them all.

In the latter years of his life (he succumbed to cancer in
2001), Yunick could be seen occasionally around media centers
at race tracks, scribbling on legal-length pads.

What many did not know at the time was that he was writing his life history. And what tales he told. When he was finished, the result was a three-volume set of largely unedited (at his behest) copy that told it like it was, at least in his eyes.

The difference between yesterday's and today's race car drivers?

"Yesterday's driver was a social disaster," said Yunick, whose legendary Daytona Beach garage was known as "The Best Damn Garage in Town."

"He drank too much and much of his time was consumed in personal problems, usually female-oriented....Hell, if you went to a hotel for a room and filled in the 'occupation' blank with, 'racer,' suddenly the hotel was out of rooms....Today's racer is a whole new ball game. Probably has the highest social rating going in all of the entertainment venues....

"Hell, a 'Winston Cupper' without a jet is hurting, the driver with a turbo-prop is looked down on. I can remember when the sign of success was when the car company of the make you race loaned you a new car to drive."

Women drivers?

"I know this is gonna piss a lot of people off, but I've never seen a good 'big time circle racing female.' I've seen females with super skill, but I never saw one that could race. No big deal as I see it; I never saw a male have a baby.'"

Don't even ask about Bill France Jr., who rated marginally lower than Bill Sr. in Yunick's estimation.

"When Billy came back from the Army, he did something that ticked me off. I was complaining about it to his dad. I said, 'It will take him five years in the fifth grade to get an idiot's license.'

"Big Bill said, 'I think he can do it in four.'" —J.M.

"Just Sign on the Dotted Line, Billy..."

When Curtis Turner and fellow entrepreneur Bruton Smith attempted to build Charlotte Motor Speedway, both got in a little deeper than they'd hoped.

In the early 1960s the two men, neither of whom really trusted the other, entered into a shaky agreement to build a $2 million track in Concord, North Carolina. Underfinanced from the outset, the venture was in deep trouble when Turner went to the Teamsters Union to ask for an $850,000 loan to complete the work. In return, Turner would attempt to organize the drivers into a union.

NASCAR president Bill France Sr. hated unions and saw them as a threat to his stranglehold on racing. He banned Turner and Tim Flock, who also was working to organize the drivers, for life.

France eventually reinstated both drivers, and Smith left racing for a few years to make a fortune in the automobile dealership business before he returned to buy out the other shareholders of the Charlotte Motor Speedway. It became the foundation for his racing empire.

But when their fate hung in the balance, France called a meeting of the drivers and mechanics—everybody except Turner and Flock—in August 1961 before a race at Winston-Salem, North Carolina.

Turner was standing outside the building where the meeting was going on, and he overheard Big Bill say that if the unions were all they were cracked up to be, he'd join himself.

"I was outside the window," Turner said later, "and I raised it up and handed him a card through the window and said, 'Here's your application.' They closed the window on me. From then on, it was just lawyers and lawsuits." —J.M. (Chapin, pp. 94)

Langley Shows the Legends How

When Ralph Seagraves, the R.J. Reynolds Tobacco salesman who was largely responsible for putting the "Winston" in NASCAR's Winston Cup, was given the honor to say "Gentlemen, start your engines!" before the first (and as it turned out, last) Winston Legends race at Lowe's Motor Speedway, the fans should have known they were in for a treat.

Instead of the traditional command, Seagraves said, "I've raced with these guys for 30 years, and there ain't a gentleman among 'em. Fire 'em up!"

What followed on the specially built half-mile track on Lowes' front straightaway was 30 laps of racing the way it used to be. Only 11 of the 22 heroes from NASCAR's past that started the race finished it, and even those cars were only recognizable by the paint schemes.

The drivers competed in modern-day race cars, but with the numbers and colors they had made famous in NASCAR's early days. When they were finished, the numbers and paint schemes were about the only thing that distinguished them from fodder for the junkyard.

With guys like Buck Baker, Junior Johnson, and Cale Yarborough in the field, who would have expected less?

Johnson, the one-time bootlegger who was known as one of the hardest-driving competitors in racing history, was involved in several skirmishes—one of which was with the pace car, which was driven by former NASCAR president Bill France Jr.

Elmo Langley raced his entire career as a field-filler, always in under-funded equipment and with only two victories in what became NASCAR's Winston Cup Series. Until 1991, that is.

Relegated to driving NASCAR's pace car in his post-retirement years, Langley had the honor of facing the best of the best one last time, and he showed them how it was done. Langley nudged three-time champion Yarborough out of the way on the final lap to take the checkered flag.

"I got Cale on the last lap, and I didn't have any reason to back off," he said.

Yarborough took the loss with more good grace than usual, saying, "He caught me napping. I didn't even see him until he passed me." —J.M

"Pops, Are We Flying Yet?"

In addition to being a daring driver, Curtis Turner's exploits in the cockpit of an airplane are equally as legendary.

One story involved his running mate "Little" Joe Weatherly, and demonstrated Turner's utter lack of fear—and maybe common sense—in the left-hand seat of anything.

It seems that once he was running late for a race at Darlington, so instead of flying his private plane into the local airport, he attempted to land it on the track's backstretch.

That was not so much a problem. Getting out was another story.

Since the backstretch of the old track was only some 1,300' long—with two-story banking in Turn 3 to clear—taking off would have been a hair-raising task even for an astronaut.

The way Weatherly remembered the story, when Turner got ready to leave, he asked "Little" Joe if he wanted to fly with him. Perhaps the only man in Christendom as crazy as Turner, Weatherly said he'd do it.

Since it would take all of Turner's concentration to get the plane off the ground in such a short space, he asked his pal if he'd take care of raising the landing gear.

Turner built up a little speed through the first and second turns, then when he hit the backstretch, he gunned it. As the plane roared down the back straightaway headed for the mountainous turn, Turner looked over at his co-pilot and asked, "Pops, are we flyin' yet?"

Weatherly looked over at the commander and replied, "I hope so. I lifted the landing gear a long time ago." —J.M. (McLaurin, pp. 117–18)

Gant Outruns Everything but the Fish

"Handsome" Harry Gant was one of the best race car drivers to ever grab a steering wheel but, as it turns out, he was not a half-bad fisherman, either. In a story passed along to veteran racing writer Tom Higgins by 1973 NASCAR Winston Cup champion Benny Parsons, Gant proved he was as handy with a rod and reel as he was with a race car.

After Parsons won the 1984 Coca-Cola 500 in Atlanta, Lou Bantle, the president of U.S. Tobacco Co. (which sponsored Parsons' Leo Jackson–owned car) wanted to reward all his drivers, which included Gant and Parsons' brother Phil, with something special. He arranged a fishing trip to a nice fishing lodge near Willingham, Alaska. What Bantle didn't know was that none of his guests were fishermen, but they were too polite to mention the fact.

On about the third day of the trip, according to Parsons, the entire party was fishing a shallow, wide part of the

Wood River, and Gant waded out to about the middle of
the run.

"He immediately begins catching rainbow trout after rainbow
trout that look about as long as your arm," Parsons said. "He's
releasing the fish after netting them.

"It gets so ridiculous that Harry starts counting, rubbing it in
on the rest of us, who aren't having anywhere near that kind of
luck. 'Twelve trout in 12 casts! Thirteen trout in 13 casts!' and
right on. He gets up to eighteen and suddenly quits fishing."

"Harry then heads toward the bank, explaining that 'There
ain't nothing to this.' Harry grinned and said, 'I'm gonna take me
a nap.'"

As Gant waded to the shore with his rod over his shoulder,
somehow or other he accidentally pushed the button on his reel
and his lure dropped into the water.

"So help me, another trout grabs that spinner and the rod tip
starts jerking down over Harry's shoulder. He spins around, sets
the hook, and starts yelling, 'Nineteen in a row! Nineteen in a
row!'

"As Harry comes by me he winks and says, 'I've got to get
out of this river. They're chasing me!'" —J.M.

chapter 3
The Lady in Black

*Southern 500 at Darlington
Raceway, 8-31-03*

Darlington Raceway is NASCAR's version of Fenway Park or Wrigley Field, a place where the history comes at you like waves crashing on the beach.

Sleep Tight and Don't Let the Bed Bugs Bite

The first Southern 500 at the track in South Carolina came on Labor Day of 1950, and seen through the light of over a half a century of NASCAR racing, it was perhaps the most pivotal stock car race in history.

In the first place, no one knew if cars right off the showroom floor would last 500 miles racing under the harsh conditions of a Sandlapper summer.

None of the drivers had ever seen a track like the 1¼ mile monster that local entrepreneur Harold Brasington had carved out of a peanut patch, much less raced on one.

But if the race had a jolting effect on racing, imagine what it meant to the townspeople who had never seen such a crowd of people. Darlington, South Carolina, was a quiet little hamlet of a few thousand souls when some 25,000 race fans poured in. The town, which boasted only one motel, was, to put it mildly, swamped.

Some of the reporters who came in to cover the race were lucky enough to find dorm rooms available at Coker College in nearby Hartsville, and there were a few motels in Florence, 10 miles away. But most people stayed wherever they found a spot to lay their heads. Hundreds slept under the stars on the town square.

Bud Moore, who owned two cars that were entered in the race—Joe Eubanks in a Mercury and Harold Kite in a Lincoln—found out soon enough that his lofty status was no guarantee of a room.

"We slept in the cars at the race track," Moore said. "We didn't have hotels and didn't have the money to pay for a hotel, anyway.

"I remember going to the hotel downtown. We went upstairs and went in the room. I turned the covers back and saw the biggest black bug you've ever seen. I told Joe Eubanks, 'Dogged if I can sleep in this bed with all these bugs.'

"We went downstairs and I told the guy behind the counter that I couldn't sleep in there with all those bugs. He said, 'Them bugs won't bite. They'll go to sleep, too.'

"We slept in the car that night." —J.M.

Joltin' Joe has Left and Gone Away...

If life was exciting for the adults in Darlington in the days leading up to that first Southern 500, imagine what it must have been like to be a kid. Especially if your dad was the man responsible for putting Darlington on the map.

Harold Brasington Jr. was nine years old when William H. G. "Big Bill" France rolled into town that summer and, being closer to the action than most, he reveled in the reflected glory.

France was a tall, garrulous man of the sort Harold Jr. had never seen. Since there were no motel rooms available any-where near Darlington, France bunked in with the Brasingtons, and young Harold must have thought he was in heaven.

For some reason, the younger Brasington said many years later, France wanted to talk to New York Yankees great Joe DiMaggio. It fell to the young boy to get him on the phone—this was in the pre-dial days, and to place a long distance call, you had to talk to the local operator.

"You can imagine how excited a nine-year-old kid was when he told me that," Brasington said. "I pick up the phone. The operator says, 'Can I help you?' I said, 'I'd like to speak to Joe DiMaggio.'

"She said, 'Honey, so would I,' and hung up."

But young Brasington was as tenacious as his dad, and he kept after the operator until she actually got the baseball legend on the phone.

"Then," he said, "I took my friends to my house and said, 'Joe DiMaggio talked on this telephone.'" —J.M.

Too Bad for Buck

Buck Baker was a city bus driver in Charlotte, North Carolina, but he also was a great race car driver. He won two NASCAR championships, in 1956 and 1957, and won the Southern 500 at Darlington three times in his career.

In the first Southern 500, however, Baker crashed his car badly in a big wreck and, for at least a few minutes, people thought he'd been badly hurt or killed.

That race was the first 500-mile race—anywhere—for stock cars. It was Labor Day weekend in the low country of South Carolina, where heat and humidity have a summer home. Some people thought cars couldn't last for 500 miles that day, and even more thought the drivers might not be able to withstand the heat for that duration.

The drivers, being a hardy lot, were determined to prove them wrong.

Most took something cold to drink with them in their cars to help them go the distance, and Baker's choice was a gallon jug of cold tomato juice.

When his car got wrecked, the first person who came to check on Baker looked inside and recoiled in horror. "No need to bother with Baker," he said. "The poor guy has had his head cut off."

Actually, Baker wasn't hurt at all. It wasn't his blood all over the place inside the car.

It was tomato juice. —D.P.

All's Well That Ends Well

Smokey Yunick, perhaps the best mechanic to ever turn a wrench in NASCAR, had his good and bad days at race tracks, but perhaps not many worse than the Southern 500 in 1957. The drivers of Yunick's two Fords, Paul Goldsmith and Curtis Turner, had qualified first and third, and all through the preliminaries, it looked as if one or the other would be a shoo-in for a victory.

The first thing that went wrong was that Yunick didn't know about a little side bet between the two.

"Our big problem was that Goldy got with a bunch of gamblers and guaranteed them he would not lead the first lap," Yunick told author Peter Golenbock for his book *American Zoom*.

"But Turner got with another bunch of gamblers out of Atlanta and he guaranteed them *he* would not lead the first lap. They come off of Turn 4, Goldy in front trying to slow down to make Turner go by him. They went across the start-finish line the first lap in the race with Goldy on the brakes with all four tires smoking, and Turner pushing him. Cotton Owens led the first lap."

Before 50 miles were in the books, Fonty Flock spun out, and Goldsmith and Bobby Myers hit him. Tragically, Myers was killed, and both Goldsmith and Flock went to the hospital. Then Lee Petty ran into Turner, sending him to the hospital. They fixed Turner's car and put Joe Weatherly at the wheel, but Weatherly could finish no better than 11th.

"That really pissed me off, because the *Saturday Evening Post* was going to give me $25,000 for my life story *if* I won the Darlington race," Yunick said.

Things got completely out of hand when Yunick tried to leave the track. Some guy in a brand new DeSoto inched his way in front of Yunick's new Ford, blocking his way.

"I jumped out of my car and went over to him and said, 'Buddy, that's a damn nice-looking car.'...I said, 'I'm hot and I'm tired. I've got to get to the hospital in a hurry.'"

Yunick said he politely asked the guy to back up, and the guy said, "Screw you."

"A state trooper was standing there looking at the whole thing," Yunick said. "I walked back to the guy in back of me and said, 'Back up a little bit.' He backed up five or six feet. I backed up and put that SOB in low gear, and I flew forward and whapped that DeSoto, and car parts flew everywhere.

"That trooper came over to the other car and he said to him, 'What the hell are you doing pulling up in front of him? Look what you did to his car. Back her up now.' Then the trooper waved me on.

"The trooper said to me, 'I was watching that thing. It was a chicken-shit deal the way he cut you off. I'm glad you whapped him.'" —J.M. (Golenbock, pp. 65)

When the Ragtops Ruled

In the 21st century, convertibles are a novelty on the highway, but there was a time in the middle of the 20th century when they were popular enough to warrant their own series under NASCAR's ever-expanding umbrella.

From 1956 to 1959, and even later at Darlington, NASCAR's Convertible Division was a popular diversion from the hardtop sedans that raced on a regular basis.

"It was the greatest idea NASCAR ever had and would not stay with it. Its timing was off, I suppose," said H. A. "Humpy" Wheeler, the president of Lowe's Motor Speedway. "I thought they were really neat....It wasn't the same old thing."

Part of the series' appeal, Wheeler said, was that fans were able to see the drivers grimacing as they fought their cars and the other competitors.

"It made the driver look very vulnerable, so therefore the convertible drivers were looked upon as cheating death," Wheeler said. "It added a dimension to it, and really it's silly, because the only difference between them and hardtops was a little piece of sheet metal."

The series was born out of necessity, since NASCAR in the late '50s had tracks clamoring for Grand National (now Nextel Cup) races, and only so many Grand National teams. NASCAR founder Bill France Sr. saw the popularity of the ragtops that were running in the Midwest under the aegis of an organization called SAFE. Soon after, he "merged" NASCAR with SAFE.

The convertible series did have its share of landmark races in its short history: Richard Petty's first race, on July 12, 1958, came in a convertible event at Columbia (South Carolina)

Speedway. The first event ever run at Daytona International Speedway was a convertible race on February 20, 1959. And what many old-timers call the greatest race ever run was the battle between upstart Fred Lorenzen and veteran Curtis Turner in the 1961 Rebel 300 at Darlington.

NASCAR discontinued the series after 1959, but France allowed the "zipper tops" (hardtops with removable tops) to run at Darlington because track president Bob Colvin was such a fan of the convertibles.

The drivers, too, loved riding in the breeze.

"I loved racing the convertibles at Darlington," said two-time Grand National champion Ned Jarrett. "Not only could the fans see the drivers, the drivers could see so much better.

"You have to remember, in those days they still had a guard rail (not a concrete wall) and you had to actually bank your car off the rail through the turns to get around the racetrack with any speed at all. Without the top, you could see just where on the rail you needed to hit it, so it was much easier. It was exciting racing."

Jim Hunter, who later became president at Darlington, was a student at the University of South Carolina back in 1959 and did not see the first ragtop race at Darlington.

"That day, I was practicing football," Hunter said. "But I listened to it on the radio, and it even *sounded* more exciting!"
— J.M.

Follow That Pace Car!

The friendship between Bob Colvin, the second president of Darlington, and driver "Little" Joe Weatherly is evidenced by the fact that Colvin named the museum he built at the track the Joe Weatherly Stock Car Museum.

But Colvin once showed his affection for the pugnacious little Virginian in a more subtle way.

The 1960 Rebel 300 race for NASCAR's Convertible Division cars was halted by rain after 74 laps on May 7, with Fireball Roberts in the lead. It was scheduled to be completed the following Saturday.

Weatherly had led but lost the lead when he pitted before the rains came. NASCAR at first said that the race would be restarted under green flag conditions, which brought protests from the drivers who had already pitted, since it would, in effect, give the non-pitting drivers a free pit stop.

NASCAR then reversed its decision, saying that the race would be restarted with five laps under the caution flag, giving the cars that hadn't pitted ample time for service.

This is where the Weatherly–Colvin friendship came in.

Colvin asked his buddy to hang around Darlington and help him promote Round 2, and all week long Weatherly could be seen on street corners in Darlington handing out little green flags to passers by.

Colvin did his part. As the driver of the pace car, all week long he'd promised fans "the fastest caution laps ever run." And he delivered.

Fortunately, the race didn't hang in the balance because Roberts was eventually sidelined with mechanical problems, and Weatherly easily won.

The punch line, however, came a few weeks later, when Colvin was traveling through another state, driving the same pace car, and was stopped by a policeman.

The officer accused him of driving 90 mph in a 30 mph zone, and when Colvin protested, the officer said, "This is the Darlington pace car and you drove it 90 mph when you should have driven it 30 mph. You cost Fireball the race and me $25 bucks that I had bet on him. So you can either post a $25 bond or go to jail!"

Colvin paid the fine without a protest. "Hell, I'd have been mad, too, if I'd lost $25," he said. —J.M. (Hunter, pp. 61–63)

Building Balmer's Box

Usually, when a race track names a grandstand or other facility after someone it's a measure of respect.

Talladega Superspeedway's Allison Grandstands is named for the first family of the "Alabama Gang." Daytona has grandstands named for Dale Earnhardt, Fireball Roberts, and Richard Petty. Atlanta Motor Speedway has its own Richard Petty and Earnhardt grandstands.

But "Balmer's Box" at Darlington was a not-so-affectionate appellation given the old open-air press box. In fact, it was not named after old-time driver Earl Balmer by the track officials at all, but by the press members in attendance at the 1966 Southern 500.

Earl Balmer, an infrequent competitor on NASCAR's old Grand National circuit during the 1960s, achieved his distinction after he arrived unannounced during the 1966 classic.

At Darlington, the press box was located in Turn 1, which offered reporters an excellent view of the start-finish line, but turned out to be directly in the line of Balmer's fire. On lap 189 of the 364-lap race, Balmer and Richard Petty tangled as their cars entered the turn. Balmer's Dodge rode the guardrail that was only about 15 feet from the press box, spewing debris and gasoline all over the 100 to 125 members of the press.

"We were diving for cover like soldiers seeking the sanctuary of a foxhole," said noted *Charlotte Observer* writer Tom Higgins.

"I thought sure as hell I was going into that press box," Balmer said. "All I could think of was, 'Oh, those poor people up there.'"

No one, including Balmer, was injured in the incident, but the press wrote up a petition before abandoning the box, demanding that track president Bob Colvin find them a safer place to sit.

"I thought I was on fire," said Benny Phillips, the reporter for the *High Point* (North Carolina) *Enterprise*. "A big piece of wood bounced off my head, and gasoline drenched me. I remember when it was over. I told them I'd beat the hell out of anybody if they lit a cigarette, providing I was still around. Luckily, nobody did."

When the reporters returned the next spring to find a more sturdy press facility, they not-so-affectionately called it "Balmer's Box" for many years. —J.M. (Fielden, Vol. III, pp. 101–2, Engel, pp. 86)

When Racing Was Racin'

Cale Yarborough's stellar career (83 wins, fifth on the all-time list) is intricately tied to Darlington Raceway and, specifically, the Southern 500.

No one was better at winning the fall classic than Yarborough. His five Southern 500 victories was the standard until Jeff Gordon tied it with his fifth win in the race in 2002. The record will likely never be broken—unless, that is, NASCAR has a change of heart and reinstates the tradition of racing on Labor Day weekend in South Carolina instead of in California.

But, according to Yarborough, there are ties and there are ties. Gordon's record at least ought to have an asterisk.

"I think Jeff ought to have to win six to equal my five," Yarborough once said, laughing, "because my first one was on the old track, and it was twice as hard to win."

Modern-day drivers consider Darlington among the toughest— if not *the* toughest—tracks on which they compete, simply because it is so difficult to drive. But Yarborough, who won on the track in 1968 before it was "modernized" by widening it in 1969, said that the before and after versions are entirely different.

In the old days, the exit off of Turn 4—now Turn 2, since the track was flip-flopped in 1997—required a driver to intentionally "kiss" the outside guardrail with his right rear bumper every lap in order to make it through the turn.

Five hundred miles of that, Yarborough said, "was absolutely nerve-wracking. And you had to touch it every lap if you wanted to be fast. The trick was in knowing how hard to hit it not to tear up your car."

In the old days, he said, the "Darlington Stripe" was a badge of honor, since the scuff marks proved a driver was getting everything possible out of his car. Since the reconfiguration, it was a sign a driver had screwed up.

In 2003, before the final Labor Day race at Darlington, Yarborough was invited to take part in a pre-race parade lap in a specially prepared race car as a salute to long-time Winston Cup sponsor R.J. Reynolds Tobacco.

He didn't exactly challenge Gordon to a match race, but well...

"It would be one heck of a last lap, I'll tell you that," Yarborough said. "I can guarantee you I'd be in the victory circle. I might have to bump him up a little bit, but I'd get it done." —J.M.

chapter 4
A Pair from the Palmetto State

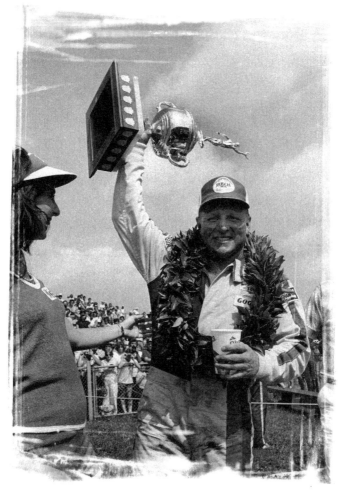

Cale Yarborough holds trophy for winning Pocono 500, 7-30-79

Two of the greatest drivers in NASCAR history came from the Palmetto State of South Carolina—David Pearson from Spartanburg and Cale Yarborough from Timmonsville.

Jim McLaurin, who has covered NASCAR throughout his career at The State in that state's capital of Columbia, has heard more than his share of stories about the two of them over the years.

"I Saw That Ocean a Minute Ago..."

Cale Yarborough had the reputation of being the toughest man
to ever drive a stock car. Listen, Yarborough was tough before
he ever got into big-time racing.

As a youth, Yarborough was bitten by a rattlesnake, hit by
lightning, and wrestled an alligator—quite by accident, but wrestled nonetheless.

Before he caught on with a big-time team in racing, he also
had a reputation as the world's worst skydiver. Yarborough and
one of his daredevil buddies—there seemed to be a plethora of
them around his hometown of Timmonsville in the 1950s—put
on thrill shows on Sunday afternoons that eventually included
jumping out of airplanes.

Skydiving had not reached the degree of sophistication that
it has today; indeed, with old Army surplus parachutes, it
involved more jump-and-hope than skill. Still, word got out about
Yarborough and Harold Lyles' derring-do, and they were hired to
jump at the Beaufort Water Festival for the munificent sum of
$50 each.

Beaufort is a small town located on the South Carolina
coast, and the two were to jump from ten thousand feet and
splash land in Port Royal Sound, where they would be picked up
by boat.

For the more experienced Lyles, that was no problem.
Yarborough had never jumped from that height, nor in such a
stiff breeze as was the case that day, and he found himself drift-
ing towards the center of town.

As he got closer, he saw that he was about to hit some
power lines, so he lifted his feet. Not enough. He climbed the

chute cords. Yarborough barely missed the power lines, but landed, of all places, on top of a dentist's office.

Yarborough was not so embarrassed by having to be rescued by the fire department, nor by landing on the dentist's office.

"I had to be the only skydiver in history who ever missed an ocean," he said. —J.M. (Yarborough, Neely, pp. 117)

"Where's Richard?"

Hall of Fame driver David Pearson may have been the coolest customer to ever drive a race car, but according to the men who raced with him, he had his moments.

In the 1976 Daytona 500, the one in which he and arch-rival Richard Petty tangled on the last lap, Pearson's calm demeanor cracked, if only briefly.

Eddie Wood, who now is a part-owner of the famous Wood Brothers team for which Pearson drove, was just another crew guy in that race.

"I was on the radio with him when he crashed with Petty," Wood recalled during a visit to the team's Stuart, Virginia, shop in 2000. Pearson didn't say a word until the pair came out of the second turn, and then he only said, "I'm gonna try him here," Wood said. When they got to turn 3, Pearson said, "I got him."

That triumph was short-lived, because Petty made his charge on the inside as they came through 3 and 4. And all hell broke loose. In those days, crews did not have TV monitors, so they were at the mercy of the crowd reaction and whatever their driver told them over the radio.

"The bitch hit me," according to Wood, was all that Pearson said.

But the "Silver Fox" quickly regained his composure: "At this time, he's spinning backwards headed toward the infield and says, 'Where's Richard?' just as calm as he could be," Wood said. "'Where's Richard?' And I said, "He's up here. He's stopped." And David says, "Well I'm coming."

The old films show Pearson's No. 21 Mercury limping across the grass and just making it back on the racetrack to take the checkered flag in one of the most exciting finishes in racing history.

At this point in the story, Len Wood, who was also on the sidelines that day, put in his two cents: "I'd just like to say something about that," he said. "Somebody comes up to Pearson after the race and says, 'Was you mad?' Pearson said, 'No, but I was getting ready to be if I hadn't won that race.'"—JM

Turtle, Tiny, and Cale

There was perhaps no odder couple in racing than when Herman "the Turtle" Beam asked Cale Yarborough to be his driver in the early 1960s.

Beam never won a race in NASCAR's top division but nonetheless held the record for consecutive finishes (84) simply because he went slow and stayed out of everybody else's way. Yarborough, on the other hand, was a disciple of Junior Johnson's philosophy: "All I want back is the steering wheel."

According to Yarborough, Beam wanted to win races, but he wanted to keep the car looking showroom new, too.

"I kept telling him that the two thoughts didn't go together," Yarborough said. "It's like telling someone they can go swimming if they don't get wet."

Neither man, however, could have anticipated what happened in the Nashville 400. Throughout the race, Beam kept flashing the message "E-Z" on Yarborough's pit board, which Yarborough of course ignored.

When the engine in Tiny Lund's Ford blew on lap 194, initiating a huge crash, Yarborough managed to miss the wreck, but not the man. Lund's car caught fire, and the 6'5", 270-pound driver leaped from his car and ran blindly across the track.

"He wanted to get away from it as fast as he could—before it blew up, I guess," Yarborough said. "He didn't see me coming down the track, and ran square into my right hand door. It didn't hurt Tiny, but it bent the whole door in."

Later, Beam told his driver: "You see there? If you'd have slowed down, he'd have missed you!" —J.M. (Yarborough, Neely, pp. 130, Fielden, Vol. II, pp. 219)

David Pearson, Meet Faron Young

At the peak of David Pearson's splendid driving career, he picked up the nickname "Silver Fox" because he drove as much with his head as his right foot.

Pearson had a reputation for letting the hotheads wear out their equipment early in the race while he coddled his along and saved it for when it counted. But even Pearson had to learn those lessons the hard way.

In his early years, he was one of the hardest chargers on the track, and that was nowhere more evident than in Atlanta in 1961, the season after Pearson won rookie of the year honors.

Pearson got in a big tangle early in the summer race and watched most of it from the sidelines. "You might say I learned a lesson that day," Pearson said later. "That was the first time I hit the wall hard on a superspeedway. I was sore for a week."

It was at about the same time that country and western singer Faron Young's smash hit—no pun intended—"Hello Walls" hit the charts, and the folks in Pearson's hometown of Spartanburg, South Carolina, drove the lesson home.

"All I heard on the radio for a week was the song, 'Hello, Walls.' This disc jockey in Spartanburg must have dedicated that song to me at least 15 times a day. Everywhere I went, people in town were asking me if I'd heard my song today. My song, they called it.

"Every time I hear that song now, it reminds me of hitting the wall." —J.M. (Hunter, pp. 80)

Excuse Me, Ma'am, Could I Borrow a Towel?

Before race car drivers owned their own private jets and stayed in their luxurious motorhomes at racetracks, they often traveled together and, on occasion, bunked together to cut expenses.

One pair that frequently buddied up was the Mutt and Jeff combination of Tiny Lund and Cale Yarborough. Before they could afford even a motel room, the 6'5" Lund and 5'9" Yarborough often slept on a mattress in the back of Lund's Pontiac station wagon.

It made for fast friends and sometimes outrageous pranks.

Once, Yarborough and Lund were staying at a motel and roughhousing in the pool after a hard day at the racetrack. Lund maneuvered Yarborough out into the deep end, where he still had solid footing and Yarborough didn't, and kept dunking the smaller driver.

Yarborough put up with it, but plotted his revenge.

When Lund went in to take a shower, Yarborough took the trash can from the room, went out to the ice machine, and loaded it up. Then he filled it with water and stirred for several minutes to achieve maximum effect, then snuck back into the room and dumped it over the top of the shower door onto Lund.

Lund, of course, bolted out of the shower and took off after Yarborough. The chase went around and around the motel parking lot until Lund, naked as a jaybird, ran smack into the proverbial little old lady, who was just getting out of her car.

According to Yarborough, she looked directly into Lund's belly button.

"' 'Scuse me, ma'am,'" he said and dashed back to his room.

Yarborough, meanwhile, watched the scene with more than a little amusement.

"The last time I saw her, she was standing there, motionless, with one hand on the car door and the other over her eyes," he said. —J.M. (Yarborough, Neely, pp. 131)

Let Me Show You How It's Done

David Pearson was not always the sly old "Silver Fox," popping up out of the weeds to win races that he looked completely out of.

Everett "Cotton" Owens, who was also from Spartanburg, South Carolina, was more noted as a car owner but was a pretty fair driver himself. He won hundreds of NASCAR modified races, and he had nine Grand National wins to his credit.

Owens had long since hung up his driving helmet when he hired Pearson in the early 1960s, but it didn't take Owens long to figure out he needed to teach him a thing or two about driving.

In 1964, he came out of retirement for one race to do it.

"It was a situation where David was young and wasn't listening to what we had to say to him," Owens said. "He'd come in the pits so wild that it would run the crew completely back over the wall, and he was losing about 15 to 20 seconds on a pit stop.

"I told him one day, 'Pearson, there's gonna come a day when I'm gonna show you I can beat you because you won't listen.'"

That opportunity came at Richmond, Virginia. Owens wound up with one more car than he had drivers for, and he didn't waste any time. Despite making his qualifying run late in the session, a definite disadvantage in those days, Owens qualified third-fastest. Pearson, along with another young colt named Richard Petty, was well back in the pack.

"They hollered up at me and told me, 'You've been out of racing so long you don't even know where the drivers' meeting is.' I stepped it off back down there and told them that I wanted them to notice how many paces I was ahead of them already. I went on and won the race, and it liked to have killed them."

Pearson did not take the loss well.

"He thought the crew had turned against him or something or another—they didn't do it right," Owens said. "It was all a part of the learning process. It's hard for a rookie coming in now to know all the secrets of getting into the pits and getting a good, quick pit stop without losing too many positions. That happened even back then.

"He was sort of upset, but he began to listen to us and he began to win races instead of giving them away."

Not that Pearson stayed young and wild. By the time he finished his career with 105 victories, Owens said he'd learned a thing or two.

"Believe me, I have seen a lot of great drivers, but I have never seen a driver who could out-drive David Pearson," he said. "He could go anywhere, anytime, and [he] could sit up front on a race track he'd never seen before. He just had that natural driving ability."

His old boss wasn't half-bad, either. —J.M.

chapter 5
The Fabulous Baker Boys

Richard Petty (left),
Buddy Baker (center)
at Winston 500 at
Talladega, 5-5-72

When NASCAR named its 50 greatest drivers as it celebrated its 50th anniversary, Buck and Buddy Baker both made the list.

At a ceremony in Daytona, each driver was introduced and given a snazzy leather jacket for being selected. They sat down in rows of chairs while the rest of the group was introduced.

The Bakers, coming as high in the alphabet as they did, had a long time to sit there. All of the drivers had put their jackets on, but Buck Baker was holding his in his lap. Buddy was trying to tell his father to put it on, but Buck wasn't having it. And Buddy just laughed about it.

That summed up their personalities perfectly.

No Punches Pulled

The late Elzie Wylie "Buck" Baker, the first man to win two consecutive NASCAR Grand National championships, was a hero of
NASCAR's rough-and-tumble days, and he had a knack for story-
telling that nearly matched his driving skills.

At the end of Baker's driving career, he operated a successful driving school at North Carolina Motor Speedway in
Rockingham and, in 1998, sat down and told a couple of tales
out of school.

Asked who his brightest pupils at the school were, Baker
said, "I guess you know who I'm going to say. Jeff Gordon and
the Burton brothers [Jeff and Ward] were about the best;
they're the ones I bring out first. You talk about the guys who
have been successful.

"To tell you the truth, I didn't see an awful lot in Jeff Gordon
until he got settled in there. He came to the school and his
mother had to rent his car for him. He could buy the company
now, couldn't he?"

Even his own family was fair game.

When asked about his son Buddy, he pulled no punches.

"When he first started out, he could tear up a damn anvil,"
Buck said. "He works with me in the school, occasionally. The
only thing about Buddy is, he hates for me to get hold of the
microphone.

"We had a bunch of executives down there and I got up and
told them they were the no-drivingest people I'd ever seen in my
life. Buddy was trying to take the mic from me the whole time. I
think they came to like it. That happened on Friday, and they
were kidding with me by the time they got ready to leave.

"There wasn't a one of them that could change gears in a four-speed transmission. I told a guy I thought I'd put automatic transmissions in 'em. A lot of the students say, 'Oh, yeah, we can drive a four-speed,' until you get 'em in there.

"When you buy a clutch two or three times a class, that gets old, you know?" —J.M.

No Fooling Around

Buddy Baker was on his way to winning the 1970 Southern 500 at Darlington Raceway, driving then for legendary car owner Cotton Owens.

"On the white-flag lap, with nothing to gain at all, I came off Turn 4 and got way sideways," Baker says. "But I made the lap, won the race, and pulled into the winner's circle."

Owens was already there.

"Cotton looked at me and said, 'I am going to tell you something,'" Baker said. "'If you had wrecked that car on the white-flag lap, if the wreck didn't kill you, I would have.'" —D.P.

Faster Than Fast

Buddy Baker won the first Busch Clash in 1979 and the Daytona 500 in 1980. He won four times at Charlotte and four times at Talladega. He also was the first driver to break the 200-mph barrier on a superspeedway, running 200.447 mph in a 1969 Dodge Daytona on March 24, 1970, at Talladega.

"I went down there for a transmission test," Baker said. "We were trying to work out a good transmission for restarts. The first lap we ran was 199.9 mph and we all said, 'Wait a minute, we may have some history here!'"

NASCAR was paid to bring in the official clocks, and Baker broke the 200-mph barrier.

"I said, 'Let's slick it up and really give them a good lap,'" Baker said. "The car would do 215; it was that good. They said I had done what I had to do. There was the 100-mph mark, then the 200-mph mark. They said, 'If you think you can run 300, we'll fix it up.' I said, 'We'd better not go there.'"

Baker was at his best on the big tracks, where he could feed his need for speed.

"The perfect driver," he joked. "A size 2 hat and a size 14 shoe."

Baker doesn't mind making himself the butt of his humor.

"The car I won the Daytona 500 in?" Baker asked. "I've often said Ray Charles could have run third in it with curb feelers on the right side. It was a pretty good car."

There's a great story there, too.

By the time Baker won the Daytona 500 in 1980, he was known to joke that he'd won the Daytona 475 three or four times but something odd had always happened to deny him the victory. Finally, he got the job done in that great car and he'd won the sport's biggest race.

"I got back to the room that night and tried to go to sleep," Baker says. "About the time I'd be just about to doze off, I'd wake up and say to myself, 'I won the Daytona 500!'"

Baker knew he wasn't going to sleep, so he decided to get up, put his stuff in the car, and make another 500-mile drive back to his home in Charlotte.

"I had just crossed the state line from Florida into Georgia," Baker says. "And I was really hauling it. I went by this state patrolman and I knew he had me. I just pulled over and waited on him."

The trooper walked up to Baker's car and recognized its driver.

"He walked up to the car and said, 'Buddy Baker, I'll declare,'" Baker says. "'I've followed your career for a long time, and you just have never had any luck. And tonight is another example of that.'" —D.P.

The Stretcher Story

Unquestionably, the all-time Buddy Baker story comes from 1967 and a race at a track in Maryville, Tennessee. Baker won the pole and knew he had a strong race car that night. He was leading by a bunch when he felt a little something funny.

"I went down into Turn 3 and I felt this little rumble," Baker said. "I thought a wheel weight had come off or something. I went down the front straightaway, and when I turned it went 'Boom!'"

His tire blew, and Baker's car went headfirst into the wall. Baker was dazed, perhaps even knocked out for a bit, and the next thing he knew an ambulance was pulling alongside his car. To this day, Baker calls the two men who got out "Bubba and Barney Fife," and they began by trying to pull Baker out of the car—headfirst—without unhooking his safety harness.

They finally helped Baker, who had broken ribs, onto a stretcher that had wheels on it and loaded him into the back of the ambulance. They forgot, however, to lock the wheels down or secure the back door. So as the ambulance tried to go up the high-banked track to take Baker out and to the hospital, the stretcher rolled into the door and the door flew open—dumping Baker onto the track.

"I'm on the gurney with my arms and legs strapped down and these cars are coming at me," Baker said. The race had not been stopped, cars were still running under caution. "I got one arm out and started waving my hand at them a little."

The cars dodged Baker, but that didn't stop the rolling gurney. Baker was still rolling down the banking, and when he rolled off the pavement the gurney's wheels dug into the mud and flipped Baker—still strapped to the stretcher—face first into the mud.

"One of the guys from the ambulance jumped out, grabbed me and rolled me over," Baker said. "He said, 'Are you OK?'

"I said, 'If I ever get off this thing, I am going to kill you.'" —D.P.

chapter 6
The Legend of
Ingle Hollow

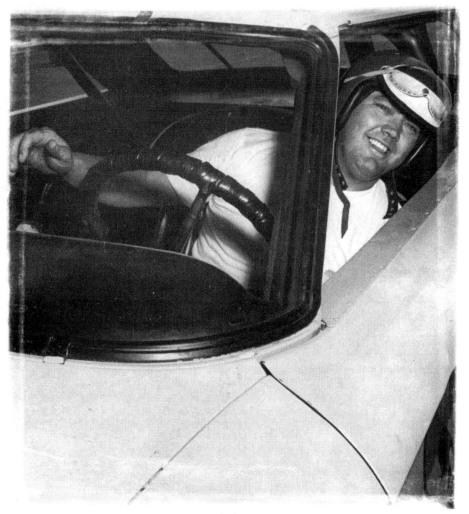

*Junior Johnson, Atlanta, 6-3-64 before
Dixie Stock Car Race*

Junior Johnson is a legend so many times over it's almost not fair.

He's one of the best drivers in NASCAR's history. Few people could do more building and working on cars. Few car owners had anywhere near as much success as Johnson had.

Beyond all of that, he might be one of the most colorful characters who has ever lived, in or out of stock-car racing.

Pop Goes the Windshield

The biggest win of Junior Johnson's driving career was a slapped-together, against-all-odds deal that was so wildly improbable that Hollywood would have never touched it. If the script writers had, however, the title would have had to have been "Gone With the Wind."

For starters, Johnson had not planned to enter the Daytona 500 because he did not have a ride. Then he was approached by car builder/owner Ray Fox with a deal. John Mansoni owned the Daytona Beach Kennel Club, the dog-racing track located just outside the year-old Daytona International Speedway, and he wanted a car in the race, cost be damned.

Mansoni, in fact, offered Fox double the going rate to build a car. Fox had a 1959 Chevrolet that could be turned into a race car, but the problem was, he had only eight days to do it, and he had no driver—until he talked Johnson into coming on board.

This was many years before race teams were large and sophisticated enough to turn out assembly-line cars, but with a handful of helpers, they got it done.

Johnson had his misgivings because the Chevrolets in that era were woefully underpowered, particularly next to the big Pontiacs, and he didn't want to go to the race just to ride around.

When he began practice, however, he discovered something that no one else had. When he was passed by a Pontiac, he found that if he could latch onto its tail, he could stay right with the faster car despite his Chevy's lack of power.

Johnson didn't know it, but he'd discovered the "bloody black art" of drafting.

"I wanted to be sure of what I'd hit on, so I went back out to practice alone," Johnson said. "The car was still the same—pretty slow." But when he found a Pontiac, "They couldn't shake me," he said. "I knew then I was right about the air creating a situation—a slipstream type of thing—in which a slower car could keep up with a much faster one. I saw this gave me a chance to win the race."

That being said, it still required a huge dose of luck.

The race was such a crash-filled melee, however, that only 39 of the original field of 68 cars finished. Most of the top Pontiacs were gone due to one circumstance or other, and Johnson found himself racing Tommy Johns' Pontiac for the win.

Johns breezed by Johnson on lap 170 of 200 and appeared headed for the win. But then, on lap 192, something curious happened.

"One of the damnedest things I ever saw on a race track," Johnson said. "The back glass popped out of Bobby's car and flew into the air. I think our speed and the traffic circumstances combined to create a vacuum that sucked that back glass right out."

The sudden change in airflow caused Johns to spin out. He did not crash, but by the time he got headed in the right direction, Johnson said, "I was long gone."

And on his way to victory. —J.M. (Higgins, Waid, pp. 48–49)

Fast Is a Relative Term

To say that NASCAR founder Bill France made racing a new game when he completed his monstrous, 2.5-mile track called Daytona International Speedway is something of an understatement.

For a bunch of guys who had cut their racing teeth on the little half-mile dirt "bull rings" that dotted the Southeast, the only "big track" they'd ever seen was the one at Darlington, and it was only 1⅓ miles around.

Daytona was a whole 'nother smoke.

Fireball Roberts' pole-winning speed at Darlington for the Southern 500 in 1959 was 123.734 mph. Cotton Owens' pole speed for the first Daytona 500, in 1959, was 143.198.

Owens' pole win at Daytona the following February was 149.892 mph, and Fireball Roberts set the top speed in qualifying at 151.556. Considering that the top speeds at most short tracks were nearly 50 mph slower than that, Daytona must have felt more like a launch pad than a race track.

In the inaugural race in 1959, only 31 of the field of 59 cars were running at the checkered flag, and in 1960, 30 of the field of 68 were in the garage at the finish, and most of the ones sidelined were due to crashes. Some said that the problem was the fact that most of the drivers were unaccustomed to the high speeds.

But there was at least one it didn't bother.

Junior Johnson, who won that Daytona 500 in 1960, said that he'd gone faster on the back roads of North Carolina when he was hauling moonshine.

"I guess that's probably the reason a lot of 'em wrecked, but the speed wasn't a problem to me," Johnson said. "See, my liquor-hauling cars were light and they had big engines....So in running a race car at Daytona, it's not like I was sitting down in something I wasn't used to.

"We were going about 150 mph at Daytona. I had run cars faster than that on the highway," he said. "I had run 'em so fast on the highway sometimes that the road ahead looked only about a foot wide." —J.M. (Higgins, Waid, pp. 49, 51)

Right on the Money

Junior Johnson grew up in Wilkes County, North Carolina, and has always lived there. He was, of course, the local at North Wilkesboro Speedway, but even he underestimated the strength of his support.

Johnson had just come back from "working for the govern-ment"—the local bootleggers' euphemism for spending some time behind bars for making moonshine—when he found himself engaged in a hot and heavy battle for a win at his home track.

During the race, something happened between Johnson and his rival that apparently did not set well with someone in the grandstands, and the guy heaved an object onto the track.

Track promoter Enoch Staley remembered it this way: "I saw something sail out of the stands and over the fence, right in front of [Johnson's opponent's] car. It hit the track and broke into a thousand pieces. It was a quart-sized fruit jar filled with white liquor.

"We were strong against anything being thrown on the track, but this was sort of amusing because of what the object hap-pened to be. I couldn't imagine a man getting so mad he'd throw away a quart of good moonshine."

Once he'd avoided the shattered glass, Johnson watched what came next with amusement.

"I saw that the law had come to the scene and was trying to arrest the guy," he said. "There was a pretty lively scuffle going on 'til the deputies got him handcuffed and took him off."

But that, according to Staley, wasn't the funny part.

"Junior didn't tell the rest of the story," he said. "The fan that got taken to jail was a feller named Ernest Money. He was Junior's uncle." —J.M. (Higgins, Waid, pp. 40)

Just the Good Ol' Boys...

It sounds like something more out of the *Dukes of Hazzard*, but Junior Johnson told it for the truth.

In the 1950s Johnson made more money hauling moonshine than he did on the racetrack, but once he made a haul that included something more than white lighting—free of charge.

It seems that Johnson and his friend Gwyn Staley were both loaded for a run to Lenoir, North Carolina. As they crossed the county line, Johnson noticed some dirt that had been kicked up in the road, so they stopped to investigate.

Out in the bushes, they discovered a car turned up on its side. It turned out that a couple of locals had been sampling some "Wilkes County Champagne" and had run off the road.

"We knew both of the guys in the car," Johnson said. "One of them was the high sheriff. They couldn't hardly stand up."

Neither man was badly hurt, but they couldn't be left where they were, so Johnson and Staley played Good

Samaritan. Each of them squeezed a man in on top of the cases of liquor in their cars, drove into town, and dropped them off—of all places—at the county courthouse. Then they went on their merry way.

"Every once in a while after that," Johnson said, "every time I'd see that sheriff, he'd kinda grin and say, 'You ain't been up the road lately, have you?'" —J.M. (Higgins, Waid, pp. 29)

The Chicken and the Pig

Junior Johnson never won a championship in NASCAR's top series as a driver. That's because he didn't run all of the races. He ran the ones he thought he could win and the ones that paid the most money.

William H. G. France, NASCAR's founder and president through its formative era, tried like the dickens to get Johnson to run a full schedule and race for a championship. At one point, France told Johnson that he needed to be committed to being a racer.

"I thought to myself, 'I am not committed to racing. I'm a bootlegger,'" said Johnson, who did, indeed, serve time in federal prison for bootlegging before getting a presidential pardon for his offense.

So Johnson came up with an analogy to make France understand his level of "commitment" to racing.

"I told him I wasn't committed, I was just involved," Johnson said. "It's like a chicken and a pig. If you're eating bacon and eggs for breakfast, the chicken is involved, but that pig is committed." —D.P.

"And Don't Let the Door Hit You..."

There's no telling how many races Junior Johnson and Bobby Allison might have won if both men had not been so hard-headed, but their short-lived run together ended just for that reason.

Richard Howard, the man who helped pull Charlotte Motor Speedway out of bankruptcy, called on Johnson in 1970 to get him to build a Chevrolet that would put the GM nameplate back at the top of NASCAR racing.

They succeeded while running a partial schedule, but in 1972, they wanted to go full throttle. To do that, they needed a couple of things: a good driver and a sponsor. In Bobby Allison, they found both. Allison had hooked up with Coca-Cola while driving for the noted Holman Moody team, but that organization folded at the end of the 1971 season.

Perfect match?

Not exactly. Both Johnson and Allison had their own ideas about how race cars should be built, and they didn't set horses from the outset. Depending on which man you ask, by midseason they weren't even speaking to each other.

Further exacerbating the situation was the fact that Allison planned to join Ralph Moody in 1973 when he formed his own team, and Johnson knew it. Add to that the fact that Johnson had a young driver named Cale Yarborough champing at the bit to get in one of his cars.

Matters came to a head at Talladega, when Allison's car started smoking due to a dripping oil line. Johnson's crew took only a few laps to repair the damage, but when they went looking for their driver, he'd already left the track.

The straw that broke the camel's back came after the season, when Allison was driving in a Trans-Am race in California. He received a 5:00 AM phone call from Howard wanting to know, in Allison's words, "Are you going to drive for us next year? If you're not, we have a chance to get the best driver in NASCAR."

"Get him," Allison reportedly said and hung up.

Johnson wouldn't confirm or deny that conversation, but noted that he'd made his mind up much earlier. According to him, Howard and Allison were talking at Rockingham that fall, trying to work something out for 1973. Allison said he'd drive, but he wanted all the sponsorship money and half of his winnings. After Talladega, Johnson had heard enough.

"I said, 'Well, he can have all the sponsorship and half the winnings. All he's got to do now is find a damn car to drive.'" —J.M. (Higgins, Waid, pp. 92, 99–101)

Junior's "Sweet Potato" Rods

R.J. Reynolds Tobacco Company (RJR) sponsored NASCAR's top series for more than three decades, and the company's marketing efforts contributed greatly to the popularity the sport enjoys today.

One of the best things RJR came up with was the circuit's all-star race, now known as the Nextel All-Star Challenge. When it began in 1985, it was called The Winston.

In that first year, the prize for finishing first in the event was $200,000. Today, it pays $1 million, but in 1985 no single race on the Winston Cup circuit—not even the Daytona 500—paid $200,000 for the win.

"This," Darrell Waltrip said, "was a big deal."

Waltrip's car owner was Junior Johnson, and Johnson was determined to win the event.

"When Junior put his mind to something you could not stop him," Waltrip said. "He would get after something with the gusto of a hungry hound. We were going to win the Winston, we were going to do whatever it takes."

One day, Waltrip went to the team's shop in Wilkes County, North Carolina, and saw Johnson himself working on something. Johnson told him it was a set of "special" rods for the motor the team would use in the all-star event.

"He called them 'sweet potato rods,'" Waltrip said. "I didn't ask him what that meant."

Johnson said it meant that they were "light and slick." He also told Waltrip that they'd be good for about 165 miles. The all-star race itself was scheduled for 150 miles, so that didn't leave much time for practice or anything else.

Waltrip, of course, won the inaugural running of the Winston.

"I passed Harry Gant on the last lap going into Turn 1 and took the lead down the back straight," Waltrip said. "I was whooping and hollering because I was one happy dude. Coming off Turn 4, if I hadn't had my seatbelt on I would have jumped out of the car. I had my hand out the window waving to the fans and about that time the motor blew all to pieces. Parts went flying for days."

Up in the broadcast booth, Mike Joy was calling the race and Neil Bonnett, who was Waltrip's teammate but was not qualified to run in the winners-only event, was working with him. Joy said that as soon as Waltrip's engine blew up, just as he crossed the finish line to win, Bonnett started hollering.

"Neil said, 'He clutched it! He clutched it!'" Joy said. "Neil was convinced Darrell had blown the engine on purpose."

He wasn't by himself. Ever since that day, Waltrip has had to listen to people accuse him of blowing up the engine so that it couldn't be inspected. Waltrip has tried to brush that aside. "The engine blew up, but it didn't disappear," he's said.

Johnson, on the other hand, is significantly more coy about what was under the hood of that car.

"They claim they checked it; they said it was legal," he said. "But I don't know what they checked."

Johnson, in fact, retired from the sport with a clear reputation for being among the most "creative" in history when it came to building cars and engines that were very close to the "edges" of the rule book.

Johnson is unrepentant.

"If you sharpen a knife, you want the sharpest edge you can get on it," he said. "That's what I did. Whenever we did something, NASCAR might get one thing but I'd keep one. I had two every time I had one. NASCAR got some of it, but they didn't get it all." —D.P.

A Language Barrier

The first time Darrell Waltrip went to Junior Johnson's shop in Wilkes County, the driver was excited and wanted to make a good impression.

"He had coon dogs in the office and race cars in his yard," Waltrip remembers. "I go in his office and there are a couple of dogs on the couch and I said, 'Is there something I can do?'"

Johnson didn't know what to do with his eager driver. But he decided to try to find him something to occupy his time.

"Junior said, 'Go out there and bounce them tires,'" Waltrip said. "Back in those days, to seat the tires on the wheel, you would take the tires and bounce them so the tire would go out against the wheel and not leak. We didn't have tubes.

"There were like 40 tires there. I didn't know how to do it, but I'd seen guys do it. So I bounced a tire and it rolled off down the hill. Another one bounced off a guy's car. I had tires everywhere."

Johnson saw what has happening.

"He [came] out of the door and said, 'Boy, what are you doing?' I said, 'I am bouncing the tires like you told me.'"

Johnson was disgusted.

"He said, 'Get them tires gathered up and get over there on the machine and get them tires bounced like I told you,'" Waltrip said.

What Johnson was actually telling Waltrip to do was "balance" the tires.

"I knew right then we were going to have a communication problem," Waltrip said. —D.P.

Take One for the Team

These days, multicar teams rule the competition in the Nextel Cup Series. With some teams spending $15 million or more just to get one competitive car on the track, having two, three, or even more teams with sponsors helping pay the bills makes it possible for the big teams to marshal all of their resources toward victory.

It has not always been that way.

There have been great multicar operations at various points in NASCAR's history.

Carl Kiekhaefer, who made his fortune in boat engines, had the Flock brothers—Tim, Fonty, and Bob—as well as Buck Baker, Speedy Thompson, and Herb Thomas all driving for him in 1955 and 1956 as his team dominated the sport. In the 1960s John Holman and Ralph Moody fielded factory-backed Fords for some of the sport's top drivers and racked up victory after victory. Richard Petty and Buddy Baker were teammates at Petty Enterprises for a while in the 1970s.

But to varying degrees, the weight of success eventually brought all of those teams down. As Robert Yates once said to Dale Jarrett when he was considering the idea of having more than one team, "The problem with having two cars is they only let you pull one car into victory lane."

If anybody was going to be able to make two teams work, it was going to be Junior Johnson, who'd already proved to the drivers he had hired that he was a master at motivation.

Darrell Waltrip joined Johnson's team in 1981, following Cale Yarborough as driver of the No. 11 Chevrolets. Yarborough had won championships in 1976, 1977, and 1978. Waltrip remembers one contract negotiating session with Johnson near the end of the 1980 season.

"I had my lawyer and Junior had his," Waltrip said. "Junior's guy was about 80 years old, and I had these guys from Connecticut who were really slick. I'd had a contract with 40 pages of all of these 'heretofores' and 'thereafters' and 'in lieu ofs,' and there was no way I was going to get out of it. But they got me out of it.

"So we're in North Wilkesboro in this little room off the side of the courthouse. Junior's lawyer is off in another little room typing up the contract and it's peck, peck, peck. It takes, like, 15 minutes to make a change. We get down the end, and it's one page. My guy was pretty slick and he thought we had a couple of bumpkins we could put something over on."

Waltrip's lawyer looked at Johnson and asked, "Junior, what are you going to do for Darrell if he wins the championship?"

Waltrip remembers what happened next.

"Junior looked down over these little half-glasses he had on," Waltrip said. "He said, 'I can tell you what I am going to do him if he don't.'"

During races in 1981, when Waltrip did win the championship, by the way, Johnson would get on the radio and urge Waltrip to drive hard. When that didn't work, Johnson would pretend to forget who was in the car.

"He'd call me 'Cale,'" Waltrip said. Yarborough and Waltrip had long been fierce rivals—it was Yarborough who gave Waltrip the nickname "Jaws."

In 1984 Johnson started a second team with Neil Bonnett driving. The teams each had shops near Johnson's home in Wilkes County, North Carolina, divided on the property by a creek. There was a little footbridge across the creek, and Johnson was just about the only guy who ever used it.

"He'd come over to our shop and say, 'Man, you won't believe the horsepower the boys over there across the creek are getting out of their engines,'" Waltrip said. "And our guys would go to work trying to get more horsepower out of our motors. He kept them racing each other harder than they raced anybody else."

Waltrip tried to get Johnson back after he'd left to join another multicar team at Hendrick Motorsports. Waltrip had been telling Johnson that Waddell Wilson was building engines with more power, and when Waltrip went to the Hendrick team, he started working with Wilson.

"Somebody asked me what the difference was," Waltrip said. "I said, 'It's like getting off a mule and getting on a thoroughbred.'"

Reporters went to Johnson to see what Johnson would say about that remark.

"I don't know anything about a thoroughbred," Johnson said, "but I did have a jackass that drove for me last year." —D.P.

chapter 7
Strange Days Indeed

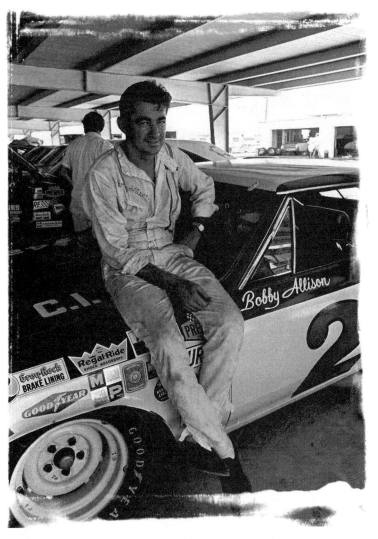

Bobby Allison

Sometimes, stuff happens for which there is no explanation...or that needs no explanation. You just have to shake your heads, move on, and remember the details for when you tell the story later.

Vroom with a View

As far as things have come in NASCAR over its more than 50 years, one thing that hasn't changed is that the only way to get a race car to a track is to haul it there.

These days, of course, the transporters that haul a team's primary and back-up cars costs upward of $250,000 and carries two cars as well as enough tools and parts to keep them on the track. It also has thousands of dollars worth of equipment teams use to make sure their cars are race-ready and serves as a team's headquarters at the track as well.

In the old days, things weren't quite so elaborate. Even the top-tier teams, like Petty Enterprises and the Wood Brothers, had flat-bed trailers that they towed behind pick-up trucks to tracks as far away as Riverside, California.

In the 1960s on one of those cross-country hauls, the Wood Brothers team had traveled from their headquarters in Stuart, Virginia, to a race at Riverside and were on their way back east when they stopped to eat. After getting back on the road, they heard a roar but couldn't figure out where it was coming from. When they pulled over, however, they figured out that it was coming from their race car on the back of their flat bed.

Sitting in the cockpit was a fan, who'd obviously been "over-served" with libations at the restaurant. The fan had the driver's helmet on and had the accelerator to the floor while turning the steering wheel. He'd climbed into the car and didn't get out before the truck took off, so he decided to make the best of it.
—D.P.

Folks, It's Just a Race!

So you think today's race fans are passionate? In 1961 at the
Asheville-Weaverville Speedway in North Carolina the fans
rioted because they believed they had been short-changed.

The Western North Carolina 500 ended in a standoff
between the fans and the racers when the race was halted after
258 laps because of impossible track conditions. The track
deteriorated to such a point that it was too dangerous for the
race to continue and, during a red-flag period brought on for the
clean up of a crash on lap 208, NASCAR executive manager
Pat Purcell told the drivers that the race would be halted in 50
laps (which, being over halfway, would make the race official),
adding, "I hope you can make it."

During those final 50 laps, the NASCAR officials slipped out
of their uniforms and quietly exited the track. When the fans
learned that 258 laps was all they were going to get, they
revolted.

A truck was dragged across the access road leading to the
infield, effectively blocking the exit. One infield denizen
approached the mob to act as a mediator, and he was promptly
heaved into a lake. Another was tossed over a fence.

Neither the sheriff's deputies nor the North Carolina
Highway Patrol was able to restore order, so as twilight
approached, Maurice "Pop" Eargle took matters into his own
hands.

Eargle, a 6'6", 285-pound crewman on Bud Moore's team,
sought reconciliation with one of the leaders of the mob and
was poked in the stomach with a two-by-four for his trouble.
Eargle grabbed the board and whacked the guy in the head.

Shortly after, the crowd broke up and the teams left. Four spectators were treated at local hospitals.

Junior Johnson, incidentally, led all 258 laps, and was awarded the 23rd victory of his career. —J.M. (Fielden, Vol. II, pp. 128)

Never Happened—Or Did It?

Sometimes the best stories around NASCAR are the ones you just can't quite nail down as to whether they're really true or not.

A great example of that involves the legend of UPS and its intentions to sponsor a race team years before it got hooked up with Dale Jarrett and Robert Yates Racing.

Supposedly, UPS had entered into negotiations to sponsor a Cup team. The talks had reached a crucial stage—it was time for the parties to exchange paperwork.

So the sponsor sent some material to the team. The team completed the forms and polished up its final proposal. All that was left was for the sponsor to agree to the final terms and the deal was done. So the team's secretary gathered up all of the material for the proposal and shipped it to the good folks at UPS.

Via Federal Express.

End of sponsorship negotiations. —D.P.

A Car on the Rocks

Maurice "Pop" Eargle was one of the most innovative mechanics on the NASCAR circuit in the 1950s and '60s, and he probably saved the lives of numerous drivers who never even knew him.

Eargle invented an ingenious but simple check-valve (a steel ball from a pinball machine, enclosed in a metal-strap cage) that kept gasoline from leaking out of the tanks of turned-over race cars.

He also invented a "rotisserie" for cars, widely copied, that allowed mechanics to work upright. When working with car owner Cotton Owens, Eargle figured that if he removed the car's bumpers and put the car on a pedestal, then locked it into place, he could rotate the car to any angle the mechanic needed.

Eargle's wizardry included building heavy-duty spindles, racing hubs, fuel and oil tank baffles, spring hangers, and dozens of other innovative pieces.

He was not above a little on-the-spot "engineering," too, when it was necessary. Once, when he was working for car owner Bud Moore, a NASCAR official on pit road measured Moore's car and told him it was too low to pass inspection. While Moore was arguing the point, Eargle, who was standing nearby, found two small flat rocks, stealthily dropped one in front of each front wheel, and rolled the car forward a couple of inches.

Then he told the official that he could have made a mistake and asked him to remeasure.

By then, of course, the car was exactly up to the standard height, and the official walked away scratching his head. —J.M.

Did Somebody Say Cut? Could They?

Most of the time in its history, NASCAR has gotten it right just about every time when it comes to marketing. The sport's incredible growth over its history has been based on a lot of good decisions.

But nobody's perfect.

On May 1, 1998, during the year in which the sport celebrated its 50th birthday, NASCAR gave itself a party in Tinseltown. It was called "NASCAR's Night in Hollywood—A Golden Celebration."

It was, well, it was just bad.

At the Wiltern Theater on Wilshire Boulevard in Hollywood, NASCAR folks rented a lot of fancy clothes and limousines and gathered for what the people putting it on tried very, very hard to make it: a grand affair.

Before the show began, the audience was instructed on how excited they should be. An announcer narrated footage of "Don Allison" and "Dave Pearson" arriving.

You knew it was going to be spectacularly bad when the opening number was—no joke—Robert Goulet and the Anita Mann Dancers performing "That's Why NASCAR is the Champ," to the tune of "The Lady is a Tramp." One snippet? "Big wreck? What the heck! That's why NASCAR is the champ."

Louise Smith, a pioneer female driver in NASCAR's history, was "honored" by Mike Love of the Beach Boys and Dean Torrence of Jan & Dean singing "Little Old Lady from Pasadena," as dancers shimmied in bikini tops while driver Morgan Shepherd joined them on roller skates.

Several awards were presented, including a lifetime achievement award to Richard Petty that was given to him by film director Oliver Stone. You could look a long, long time and not find two men who had less in common, politically or culturally.

"It was something different," Petty said.

Somebody asked him if it was like an out-of-body experience.

"Not out of body," he said, "but definitely out of place." —D.P.

Keep Reaching for the Stars

For more than a quarter of a century, NASCAR races did not start without the approval of Johnny Bruner and, remarkably, all but one of those races finished with his approval.

The Birmingham, Alabama, native's first involvement with racing came in 1937 when he worked as an assistant flagman for midget races at a small New Jersey track, and he found the job to his liking.

"I never got to drive; it just never interested me," he said. "I always wanted to be a starter and nothing else."

His big break came in 1949 when Bill France Sr. asked him if he'd help by flagging the beach races at Daytona. It began a lifelong friendship and a very interesting career.

Back in those days, most flagmen worked the race from trackside instead of in flag stands, and Bruner had his share of moments. He was occasionally bowled over by the midget racers, and he had his feet run over more times than he'd have liked.

But the 1952 beach-road race at Daytona had enough excitement to last him for a while.

"I'll never come any closer to getting the real checkered flag myself than that day," he said. "I had just finished flagging Marshall Teague's winning car when the fourth-place car, driven by Tommy Thompson, lost control. That big Chrysler headed toward me from about 200 yards out, and I started backing away more as a reflex action than anything else."

Bruner almost had it figured out, thinking that the car would drift away out toward the sand dunes, but the tail end caught the pole that held up the start-finish line banner, and it careened wildly in his direction. He didn't have time to run, so he jumped.

"Always jump when something is about to hit you," he said. "Never get caught with your feet on the ground."

Thompson's car hit him and knocked him about 40 feet into the air, but he was uninjured.

"I got up with the flag in my hand and still chewing on my cigar," he said. "I guess Gabriel wasn't quite ready to flag me off for good." —J.M. (Cutter, pp. 95)

"Say What, Bobby?"

There is nothing funny about the crash that robbed veteran driver Neil Bonnett of his livelihood in 1990 at Darlington, nor in the wreck at Pocono Raceway in 1988 that ended Bobby Allison's driving career.

But Bonnett, who later lost his life in a crash while trying to make a comeback in the 1994 Daytona 500, recovered from the near-fatal injury at Darlington, and he once noted that his and Allison's recuperation period did have its moments.

Allison's head injury at Pocono was so severe that he spent months in the hospital and years in recuperation from brain damage. Bonnett suffered temporary amnesia after he wrecked at Darlington and, since he and Allison were both from

Hueytown, Allison was the first to check in on his friend and protégé.

The scene, Bonnett recalled later, was poignant, but not without some levity.

"Bobby was the first guy who stopped by my house," Bonnett said. "We were sitting there on the couch. Between Bobby trying to say what he was thinking and me trying to remember what he was saying, it was a helluva conversation." —J.M.

Everything's Bigger in Texas

It might not be in the record books, but the worst traffic jam in the history of motorsports took place in 1997 at Texas Motor Speedway on the morning of the track's first Cup race. People who go to a lot of races gripe about traffic all of the time. But this one was…well…it was just plain biblical.

Imagine traffic on a scale. Zero is an open road. Three is rush hour. Seven is a 20-car pileup. Ten is when a passenger jet makes an emergency landing in rush hour at the intersection of two interstate highways and causes a 20-car pileup. On that scale, the first Texas race was a 50.

To be fair, it wasn't totally the track's fault.

Heavy rain fell for days before the race. On the first day of practice, at one point teams were told to put down all of the lift gates on their haulers and put away all of their equipment because big storms were coming. The radar looked like someone had spilled red paint on it. When the storms arrived that afternoon, they were open for business.

The result of all that rain was that almost all of the parking lots surrounding the track, expect for a few thousand paved spaces immediately adjacent to the track, were unusable. The track, which has nearly 170,000 seats, planned for fans to park in fields around the property. But those field were simply too muddy to use.

Everybody knew it was going to be a problem, and the track and local officials tried to line up bus service to shuttle people from useable lots several miles away. But it was the first time any kind of crowd that size would be coming to the track, and even under ideal conditions there would have been some first-time confusion.

This, however, was not ideal.

At 8:00 AM on race morning, traffic was already backing up in virtually every direction and on virtually every road leading to the track, which is located north of Fort Worth. By 10:00 AM, Interstate 35-W, which goes right in front of the track, had turned into a parking lot. People were pulling their cars off to the side of the road, getting out, and walking toward the track. It was faster. The buses that had been arranged to get people to and from the satellite parking lots were stuck in traffic, too.

It's amazing anybody got there that day. It's even more amazing that anybody came back the next year, too, after having to deal with that.

The track itself got its own criticism.

As first designed, Texas Motor Speedway had compound banking. It was relatively flat in the low groove, then banked more steeply in the second and third lanes up. The idea was for Indy-style cars to run on the flatter surface and stock cars to use the higher banking, but the transitions between lanes proved tricky.

There also was a "kink" in the outside wall coming off Turn 4. As cars exited the turn, the wall seemed to almost stick out into the outside groove. From the first time you saw the track, you couldn't help but think how odd it seemed. And drivers complained about it.

So in 1998, when the teams were getting ready to come back for the second year, there was a lot of talk about what might happen. The week before the race, there was talk in the garage area at Bristol Motor Speedway that NASCAR had considered postponing or canceling the race because it had once again been rainy that spring and the track had drainage problems that caused water to seep up through cracks in its surface. One story making the rounds was that when track management drilled a hole to try to assess the problem, a 10-foot high geyser of water sprung out.

"That's the most insane thing I have ever heard," track general manager Eddie Gossage said.

Gossage said there had been some drainage issues that prevented some teams from testing, but ditches had been dug to address the problem. And he was getting a little tired of hearing his track criticized roundly.

"I am not taking a shot at Las Vegas or California or anybody," Gossage said of tracks that were also new at the time. "They are fabulous race tracks and great additions to the circuit.

"But the Blue Angels flying team is exciting because their wing tips are a few feet apart. If they were a half-mile apart, it wouldn't be as interesting."

Early in the week of the 1998 race, Gossage revealed that his track's souvenir department had come up with a new T-shirt. "I expect it to be the first one to sell out this weekend," Gossage said.

On the front, the shirt said, "No Crying." On the back, it said, "Shut up and Drive."

You know where this is going, don't you?

That Friday, there were several crashes in practice for both the Cup and Busch Series, and there were so many crashes in the Busch qualifying that Cup time trails were 90 minutes late getting started. By that time, Turns 1 and 2 were already covered in shade by the grandstands. Early on in the Cup qualifying session, Derrike Cope crashed in that area. Then Lake Speed wrecked.

The next thing you knew, NASCAR officials were standing out in Turn 1 putting their hands and napkins and handkerchiefs down on the racing surface. And they were feeling water seeping up through the asphalt.

Qualifying was postponed until 10:15 AM Saturday.

"What has happened, we believe, is that the race cars form a suction on the race track as they go by and they're pulling [moisture] out as the day goes on," Gossage said. "Once the sun set, it quit evaporating. Plus, we've had 10, 20, 30 cars on it at a time. Now we've got one at a time, so the cars can't dry it as well.

"That's the dilemma we face. It's the first time we've seen this in about a week or 10 days. It's extremely regrettable…but those are the cold, hard facts."

The cold, hard reality, though, was that the drivers were not happy.

"What's frustrating is the drivers posted some concerns about it and hoped they'd listen," Jeff Burton said. "All we get is them printing T-shirts about it saying we need to shut up and drive. That's frustrating."

Ken Schrader was even more blunt. "It isn't going to get fixed without bulldozers," he said. "Not the whole race track, but it needs major work. I don't care what they say."

After that weekend, the track was reshaped. It has been repaved again since, and in the past few years complaints about the track surface have abated.

But those first two years were something to remember.

Going back to that first race in 1997, one of the most unforgettable moments came just minutes before the green flag flew. The track had arranged to have famed concert pianist Van Clyburn perform the national anthem that day. A singer had been booked to do "Yellow Rose of Texas" before that, but after he sang that song he was re-introduced to do the anthem. As he sang, those watching from the press box and suites atop the grandstands could see a flatbed truck driving through the infield with a grand piano on it. The seat was empty.

The singer forgot part of the words to the "Star-Spangled Banner," but in his defense he didn't know until a few minutes before he started singing it he was going to be asked to.

Where was Van Clyburn?

No, he wasn't caught in traffic. Track officials figured that might happen, so they arranged to have a helicopter pick Mr. Clyburn up and bring him in for the pre-race festivities. Well, at least they were supposed to.

Somebody forgot to arrange for the helicopter. —D.P.

chapter 8
The Family Business

*Richard Petty, after
winning Daytona 500,
2-14-71*

The Pettys. The Allisons. The Waltrips. The Earnhardts. The Bakers.

Stock-car racing's history is filled with stories about the sport's famous families.

Honor Thy Father and Mother...
Particularly Thy Father

Richard Petty, the "king" of NASCAR racing with 200 victories, is probably the most graceful man to ever wear a racer's fire suit.

In the middle of his remarkable 1967 season, when he won 27 of 58 events and became NASCAR's all-time winningest driver with 55 victories, it was his father Lee Petty's record that he broke.

Appropriately enough, the 55th win came in the Rebel 400 at the legendary Darlington Raceway, and perhaps more appropriately, the guy who finished second that day was David Pearson, whose 105 career victories would put him in second place behind Petty in career wins.

Despite running into the wall on lap 89 of the 291-lap race, Petty led 266 laps and was more than a lap in front of Pearson at the finish.

When he became NASCAR's all-time winningest driver that hot afternoon in the South Carolina flatlands, his post-race comments were about as graceful as they come.

"There's been a lot of fuss lately over me tying or breaking Daddy's record of 54 victories," Richard Petty said. "We've never even thought of it that way. As far as we're concerned, the Petty family has 109 wins." —J.M. (Fielden, Vol. III, pp. 140)

Check, Please!

Nearly all of the parties involved in the glorious fight after the 1979 Daytona 500 have gotten a ton of mileage out of what many call one of the landmark races in NASCAR history.

Bobby Allison, in fact, says that by his estimation NASCAR has made $53 billion off of what happened after the first Daytona 500 to be shown on live network television.

Donnie Allison and Cale Yarborough wrecked each other on the final lap, allowing Richard Petty to go by and win the race. Bobby Allison pulled his car up to where they'd stopped when the race was over, saying he wanted to see if his brother needed a ride back to the garage. "But then Cale accused me of causing the wreck, and I think I questioned his ancestry," Bobby Allison says. "In fact, I am sure I did."

Bobby Allison said Yarborough came at him and hit him in the face with his helmet, sending blood gushing from Allison's face.

"I had to get out of the car an address it, or run from him the rest of my life," Bobby said. "So I climbed out and my story is he started beating on my fist with his nose."

Yarborough's line is that it wasn't a fair fight—he believed he should have had one hand tied behind his back to fight the two Allisons.

Junior Johnson owned the car Yarborough destroyed in the wreck, and he was a little put out. "I knew what went on out there," Johnson said. "And after it was over, somebody came running up to me in the garage after they wrecked and said they were over there fighting.

"I was asked if I intended to go over there and do some-thing about it. I said, 'Hell, no, let 'em kill each other as far as I'm concerned. The day is over for me!'"

Afterward, NASCAR fined Yarborough and both Allisons $6,000 each for their "actions detrimental to racing," which, given what the incident means to the sport's lore, makes that a fairly laughable phrase.

Prize money in 1979 wasn't what it is today. Two years before that, Allison ran 30 races and earned a total of $94,575 in official winnings. In 2005 Bobby Labonte finished 43rd in the Daytona 500 and won $276,444—almost three times Allison's 1977 annual total.

"We got fined $6,000 apiece," Bobby Allison said. "Donnie and Cale won more than that but I finished 11th and didn't make enough to pay the fine. I had to write a check."

Allison's official winnings that day were $17,725, but after car owner Bud Moore got his share, Allison swears he didn't have $6,000 to pay the fine.

"They refunded the money after we were good boys for the designated amount of time after that," Allison contends. "But they only refunded the prize money they withheld and they never gave me back the check I wrote." —D.P.

Goats, Grass, and Going Fast

It seems that Dale Jarrett almost tried as hard to get out of being a race car driver as his father, Ned, tried to be one. Both of them, however, wound up being NASCAR champions.

Ned Jarrett was the part owner of a race car that ran at Hickory Motor Speedway. His parents didn't mind him owning and working on race cars, but they didn't care for the idea of him being a driver. Race car drivers of that day were know as bootleggers and roughnecks, and those reputations weren't always that far off.

John Lentz, Jarrett's brother-in-law, was driving the car. But one night he got sick, and they decided that Ned should drive the car. Ned did so, without telling anybody, and finished second. Jarrett and Lentz decided that Ned might be a better driver than Lentz, so the next week Jarrett drove again, once again under Lentz's name. He won that week, and when his father found out about it, he told Ned that if he was going to drive he should try to win and certainly should take the credit for it when he did.

So Ned Jarrett officially started his driving career. But it was hardly a lucrative profession, and in 1957 when he wanted to buy a race car that Junior Johnson had driven for $2,000, he was a little bit short. He was, to be exact, $2,000 short.

He had no money in the bank, but after 5:00 PM on a Friday he gave the car's owner a personal check for $2,000. There were 100-mile races that weekend in Myrtle Beach, South Carolina, and Charlotte, and Jarrett knew that if he won both of them he might come close to covering the check. He did win both races, earning $1,900. He scraped together the remaining $100 and got to the bank bright and early Monday morning.

Ned Jarrett would go on to win 50 races, but he retired as a driver at the age of 33 and went back home to Hickory, North Carolina, where he started promoting races at the track where he'd first raced.

Running Hickory Motor Speedway became the Jarrett family business. But his son Dale was a teenager with other ideas about his life. He'd been a star athlete in high school, playing baseball, football, basketball, and golf. He also had been offered a golf scholarship at the University of South Carolina but decided against going to college. He'd been married and had a son and, at age 20, needed a job. So his father hired him to work at the track.

The younger Jarrett did everything from selling popcorn to driving the pace car at Hickory Motor Speedway, but one of his least favorite jobs was cutting the grass. He decided that what Hickory Motor Speedway needed was some goats to eat the grass he didn't want to cut.

It seemed like a good idea at the time, Dale would say years later. And the goats did eat grass. They also, however, took a liking to the seats and dashboards in some old cars Ned kept on the track's grounds for use in demolition derbies.

"You could say I lacked direction," Dale admits.

At about the same time, he started working on a car that two of his buddies, Jimmy Newsome and future NASCAR crew chief and car owner Andy Petree, had been working on. They wanted to race it at Hickory, but they needed a race engine. Dale asked his father to loan them the money to buy it, and because of that, Dale was elected to be the team's driver.

That first race was a revelation. Dale Jarrett started 25th and finished ninth, and after the race, 1970 NASCAR champion Bobby Isaac came down pit road and found Ned.

"I thought you said Dale was driving that car tonight?" Isaac said.

"He was," Ned said.

"Can't be," Isaac said. "He was too smooth."

Dale Jarrett got out of the car and started looking for his parents. He wanted to tell them that he'd just decided what he wanted to do with his life. —D.P.

Like Father, Like Sons

Buddy Parrott remembers the day he fired his son.

"One morning, I heard the most awful squealing sound I have ever heard in my life," Parrott said.

It was 1984, and Parrott was crew chief for Richard Petty at Curb Motorsports.

Soon after the squeal, his secretary hurried into his office. "She had the most beautiful fingernails," Parrott said, "but they were just covered with grease. She was crying, 'Look at my hands!'"

A prankster had squirted grease under the handle on a file cabinet. When the secretary went to pull out the drawer, she came out with fingers full of goop. Parrott called a team meeting, demanding to know who was to blame.

"They were all looking around, and I was looking to see who the heck had done this," Parrott said. "One of them had a little sheepish grin on his face. I knew without even asking, it was Todd Parrott."

That day, Buddy Parrott taught Todd the meaning of a word that Buddy had learned early on during his racing career.

"I've had the opportunity to work with a lot of people," Buddy said. "They came out with this word—'fire,' as in 'getting fired.' That gave me the opportunity to switch around. I got fired, I got rehired."

Buddy rehired Todd a few days after the Great Grease Caper in 1984, and the family has done okay since.

When Jeff Burton got his first career victory in the inaugural Cup race at Texas Motor Speedway in 1997, Buddy Parrott was his crew chief. It was the 45th career victory for Parrott, who has since retired.

Todd worked at Curb and then with Blue Max Racing and Penske Racing South before joining Robert Yates Racing in October of 1995. He served as crew chief for Ernie Irvan for the final two races of that season, then helped Dale Jarrett win a championship. In 2006, Parrott will be crew chief for Bobby Labonte on the No. 43 Dodges owned by Petty Enterprises.

"I grew up in the sport," Todd Parrott said. "When I was growing up, when we were going to Talladega, I would go down a week early and go to Hueytown to spend the week with the Allison boys. I would hang out with Davey and Ronald, Donald and Kenny Allison—Donnie's boys."

Buddy Parrott was a crew chief even before he got the family started in racing.

He grew up in Charlotte and went to races with his buddies, but he also had a job working for Pritchard Paint and Glass Company.

"I was a glass mechanic for nine years," he said. "I had a crew that I worked with, and I got myself up to crew chief there. So, I was a crew chief before I was a crew chief."

Parrott's company opened a new store in Salisbury and he got a chance to move there. In 1968, he met Ross Huggins of Huggins Tire, a company that sold tires to race car drivers.

"Ross and I just hit it right off. He was my kind of guy, the kind who worked hard and played hard," Parrott said. He went to Daytona with Huggins' company that July.

Buddy said he came home and told his wife, Judy, that he was going racing. She thought he meant as a fan. He didn't.

Young Todd was four years old. His brother Brad—who is now a crew chief for the Busch Series team run by Roush Racing for driver Carl Edwards—was still a toddler. All of a sudden, Dad was off driving a tire truck to a different race track each weekend. What followed might diplomatically be called a period of adjustment.

"I came home from Bristol one time, drove the tire truck back," Buddy said. "I opened the door and I said, 'Hello!' The house said, 'Hello!' back, echoing through the rooms. I walked in and there was nothing there. She had moved back to Charlotte and moved everything out. She had just had enough of all of this racing."

Racing did take a toll, Todd Parrott said. "At first, Mom and Dad had a hard time with their relationship because Mom didn't understand why he had to be gone all of the time," Todd said. "When I was growing up, he was gone a whole lot. We didn't get to go to baseball games and stuff like that and spend time together with me growing up. I don't have any resentment about it, but I didn't get to know my dad like a lot of people do."

Buddy and Judy Parrott were separated for about a year, then put things back together. Judy came to understand the sport that had a hold on her husband and was pulling her sons toward it. She eventually helped form a public relations company that handled race teams, and racing truly became the family business.

Todd chose racing over a possible career as a golf pro. "After graduation, I thought, 'Man, what am I going to do now?'" he said. "I had two or three small colleges call and offer me scholarships to play golf. But I was the kind of person who liked playing golf and I didn't like the books."

Todd continued his education, however, learning how to make cars go fast.

"I had the best teachers in racing to learn from," he said. "Barry Dodson, Jimmy Makar, Rusty Wallace, Robin Pemberton, I can't say enough for what they did for me."

While Todd was learning the ropes, Buddy was finding success as crew chief for Bob Whitcomb's team with Derrike Cope as the driver. They won the Daytona 500 in 1990.

Their careers crossed paths again when both worked at Penske South. Buddy came on as crew chief in 1992 and was there for the following two seasons. That team won 19 races. Wallace finished second in the 1993 points race, losing to Dale Earnhardt by 80 points.

"One night late, I was putting a carburetor together and he [Todd] broke something off on it, something I had asked him not to do," Buddy recalled. "I think it was a 4' level that I threw at him. Everybody still says it sounded like a helicopter taking off as it went over the top of his head going whoomp, whoomp, whoomp."

Parrott's first full season as a crew chief could not have started better. Jarrett won the 1996 Busch Clash and came back a week later to win the Daytona 500. —D.P.

Davey Allison Goes to School

Bobby Allison looked at the young fellow sitting beside him during the post-race interview following the 1988 Daytona 500 and grinned. Then he asked the question that was on everyone's mind: "What I want to know is, would you have passed your dad if he'd let you?" the elder Allison said.

Davey didn't blink. "Without a doubt," he said. "Without a doubt."

One of the most compelling things about auto racing is that it is one of the few sports in which brothers compete against brothers on a regular basis, and occasionally, fathers against sons. But seen through the prism of time, the battle between Bobby and Davey Allison that February afternoon was a classic in every sense.

Bobby Allison was only a few months away from having a crash at Pocono, Pennsylvania, that would end his racing career, and young Davey's star was just beginning to rise. Accidents that would take the lives of both Davey and his brother Clifford were years away, and the future never looked rosier for the Allison clan.

There had been other father-son match-ups. Buck Baker regularly roughed his boy Buddy up whenever the two were on the same track, and Lee Petty never gave Richard a break when the two were fighting for a position. Richard, in his turn, never cut Kyle Petty any slack.

There had been two father-son 1–2 finishes (with Lee Petty beating Richard twice) prior to the Allison's duel at Daytona. But in most of those instances, the fathers held the upper hand, both in equipment and racing savvy, and the battles were more skirmishes than fight-to-the-last-ditch struggles.

Behind the wheel, the Allisons were as close to equals as you could get.

The Daytona 500 was, and is, the biggest stage in stock car racing. The winner's name is automatically included in any list of racing's great drivers. Bobby's name was already on that list, twice, and that week in 1988 he had won every race in which he was entered at Daytona.

The sense of drama on Sunday was heightened when Davey Allison crashed his car in the final practice on Saturday afternoon, and his crew worked most of the night to get it back into shape.

It was a great race and a great finish. Bobby stood off a last-ditch attempt to pass by his son and beat him by 2½ car lengths at the checkered flag. No chicanery, no blocking out. Just outrunning.

"My whole career, I've done my best to play it straight," Bobby said. "And when you are racing against the best young-ster to ever come along, you wouldn't want to do anything other than that."

Still, Davey wondered aloud what might have happened if his car hadn't been damaged on Saturday. Bobby, eyeing the 30-race campaign ahead, looked at his son and grinned.

"You've got 29 more times this year to find out," he said.
—J.M.

chapter 9

Life in Technicolor

*H.A. "Humpy" Wheeler
(right) with Elliott Sadler*

Lowe's Motor Speedway president H. A. "Humpy" Wheeler likes to tell people that a race promoter's job is to provide a little "Technicolor" for people who lead black-and-white lives.

If stock-car racing has a P. T. Barnum, it's Wheeler. Once, in fact, he heard a couple of sportswriters griping about one of his lavish pre-race extravaganzas. "They might as well have a circus," one said. The next year, the pre-race show was, literally, a circus.

One Must Die

Humpy Wheeler remembers going to sports events when he was a kid and being bored as he waited on the game or the race to begin. He never could figure out why there was nothing going on.

He's always tried to remember that, he says, in his career as a track promoter. There's almost always something going on somewhere at Wheeler's track.

Most of his ideas are good ones. Some of them, however, don't work out. There was, for example, the time he tried to break the world record for assembling the world's largest marching band. He invited high schools to send their bands to his track before a race, and dozens of them did. There were hundreds and hundreds of teenagers all over the place, all decked out in their full uniforms—many of which were woolen.

As it turned out, the day of the race came up sunny and very, very warm. And as the bands stood on the track waiting for their part of the program, it got pretty hot in those wool uniforms. Too hot, in fact, for some of the students.

"They were dropping like flies," Wheeler said.

Wheeler also liked having a swimmer from the little town he grew up in, Belmont, North Carolina, come over to the track during race weeks and try to break world records. The swimmer, whose nickname was "Moon," was actually a specialist in treading water. For hour after hour, Moon would tread water. And he'd do it longer than anybody ever had.

It was quite an accomplishment, no doubt, but it frankly was not terribly thrilling. Wheeler was looking for a little something to spice up Moon's act, and he was talking to his staff about it one day in a meeting.

"I know," one of his assistants said, "let's put a shark in there with him. You know—Moon versus the Shark: One Must Die!"

The movie *Jaws* was out and everyone got a big laugh out of the suggestion. But Wheeler wasn't laughing. The idea, he thought, had merit. His staff was mortified. "We can't do that!" they insisted.

Wheeler wasn't crazy. But he was thinking outside the box. "We could put him in a chain mail suit, couldn't we?" he said.

Eventually, the staff won out. And Moon never had to face the shark. —D.P.

Head Games

Buddy Baker had started driving for car owner Ray Fox and he was looking for that little bit extra that he hoped would help him become a winning NASCAR driver. Humpy Wheeler convinced Baker that some extra physical conditioning would do the trick. Wheeler, who'd been an amateur boxer, convinced Baker that they should do some sparring. Wheeler told Baker that if they worked out every day for two weeks leading up to an October race in Charlotte, he guaranteed that Baker would win the race.

The weather still can be rather warm in the Carolinas in October, and it was that year. Still, Baker and Wheeler would turn the heat up in their car as they rode to a field where they would run a little and then spar a little. Baker says his pants were getting too big for him and his stomach was getting harder and harder.

On the day before practice for the Charlotte race began, Wheeler and Baker had one last workout planned.

"Just was we were going to start working out he said, 'No hitting in the head,'" Baker said. For two weeks, nobody had hit anybody in the head, so Baker thought that was odd. It seemed even more odd when the first time Wheeler took a swing, he hit Baker in the right ear.

"When he did, I was like, 'Okay, let's go,'" Baker said.

Baker and Wheeler went at it, chasing each other through the field and across the road into a man's yard.

"About that time, Humpy put his gloves up and said, 'We'd better stop before somebody gets mad,'" Baker said.

"I said, 'To hell with you, I've been mad since we left that field over there!'"

That was the end of the fight.

But Baker won the race that week. —D.P.

Let There Be Lights

On their own, Humpy Wheeler and T. Wayne Robertson each had their brilliant moments. Put them in a room together, however, and something memorable was almost bound to happen.

Such was the case at a 1991 meeting in Robertson's office in Winston-Salem, North Carolina. But that's getting ahead of the story.

Wheeler is president of Lowe's Motor Speedway at Charlotte and, since shortly after he was out of college at the University of South Carolina, he's been in the stock-car racing business in one form or another.

Early on, for instance, Wheeler was running Robinwood Speedway, a dirt track in Gastonia, North Carolina. One weekend his water truck broke down and Wheeler was in desperate need of a tanker he could use to prepare the racing surface. He called a buddy who worked for a septic tank company and borrowed that truck, but at the race that night, his patrons couldn't help but notice the pungent residual odor the truck had left behind. Wheeler took to the track's public address system and blamed the smell on an unprecedented wind shift that was carrying the odor in from a nearby pulp mill, which, of course, was not really nearby at all.

Robertson, meanwhile, started out in the marketing arm of R.J. Reynolds Tobacco Company as a driver of one of the "show" cars that goes around to supermarket openings and things of that nature to promote the company's sponsorship of NASCAR's top series.

With boundless enthusiasm and a knack for tackling every challenge as though it were a great opportunity, Robertson moved up through the ranks and wound up as president of Sports Marketing Enterprises. No idea was too big, no plan too grandiose for Robertson if he thought it would help NASCAR and the Winston Cup Series grow and gain acceptance.

One story about Robertson sums up his approach to life. One day he was trying to get into Atlanta Motor Speedway to take part in the pre-race ceremonies, but he was stuck in traffic. Robertson "urged" his driver to circumvent the normal pattern set up for ingress to the track, so they were heading down the median when a local traffic enforcement officer took notice...and umbrage.

The officer pulled over Robertson's car and headed over to speak to the driver. But he never got a chance. Virtually before the car was stopped, Robertson bounded out.

"Where have you been!?" Robertson asked. "We've been looking for you for miles!"

The officer was flummoxed, having no idea what Robertson was talking about.

"You're our escort, right? We've got to get inside that track so they can get this race started on time," Robertson said.

The officer bought the bluff and Robertson not only had permission to bypass the traffic he'd been fighting, but he also had help doing it.

In 1985 Robertson and his RJR staff came up with the idea of a big-money all-star event for NASCAR's top series. The inaugural event was set for May at Wheeler's track in Charlotte, and the hype was right down Wheeler's alley. It was a big success, too, with Darrell Waltrip winning the inaugural event.

The idea was to move the race around to different tracks, the way other sports put their all-star games in various places. The second year, it was scheduled for Mother's Day at Atlanta Motor Speedway. That's the day everyone in NASCAR discovered that it wasn't a good idea to race on Mother's Day. The joke was that it would have taken less time to introduce the fans to the drivers than it would have to introduce the drivers to the fans.

So the all-star event returned to Charlotte in 1987 and staged one of the most memorable events in NASCAR history—known for Dale Earnhardt's "Pass in the Grass" where he maintained the lead (it never was actually a pass) despite being run across the corner of the infield grass in the track's trioval.

That was the first year of a five-year contract between RJR and the Charlotte track, a deal that ended with the 1991 running of the Winston.

And that brings us to the aforementioned meeting in Robertson's office in 1991.

It was time to negotiate a new contract. Robertson, frankly, wasn't sure the all-star race needed to continue anywhere. He was afraid it had lost its sizzle but was willing to listen to Wheeler's ideas. Wheeler had a lot of ideas. But he could tell that none of them were doing anything to capture Robertson's imagination.

"I kept throwing things at him, and nothing was getting to him," Wheeler said.

Until, that is, the light went on.

Actually, until the lights went on.

Wheeler told Robertson that he wanted to hold the all-star event on a Saturday night, under the lights. It was a return to racing's roots since short tracks had long run under the Saturday night lights. Robertson loved the idea.

What made Wheeler's idea so revolutionary was the fact that no track as large as the 1.5-mile Charlotte track had lights.

Until the moment the words came out of Wheeler's mouth, his staff had no idea Wheeler had planned to propose lights for the track. There was a good reason for that—Wheeler thought of it on the spot.

"I told them I didn't have the slightest idea how we were going to do it, but we were going to do it," Wheeler said.

The trouble was that lighting a track the size of Charlotte was a considerably more difficult matter than simply putting up light posts. Cars enter the track's turns at better than 180 mph, and at that speed any pockets of dark and light appear as strobe lights—and that wouldn't work. Glare and shadows were also potential issues.

Wheeler had some ideas, including a wide band of light placed atop the wheel fence. He set up a test in Turn 1 and then realized he had a problem.

"I brought a bunch of people in," Wheeler said. "We were going to test in the pace car, and everybody was looking at me like, 'Who's going to do this?' I had to do it, and I almost killed myself. I went down into the first turn and, I'm telling you, I couldn't see anything."

Eventually it took Musco Lighting, a company from Iowa that specializes in stadium lighting projects, to provide a solution. The company built a one-fourth scale model of Turn 4 at the Charlotte track in an airport hangar near its headquarters to test the system it invented, which features lights bounced off mirrors. Musco wound up getting more than a dozen patents for things it invented to complete the system.

"As soon as I saw it, I said, 'How simple!'" Wheeler said. "I knew it would work." —D.P.

chapter 10

Gone Too Soon

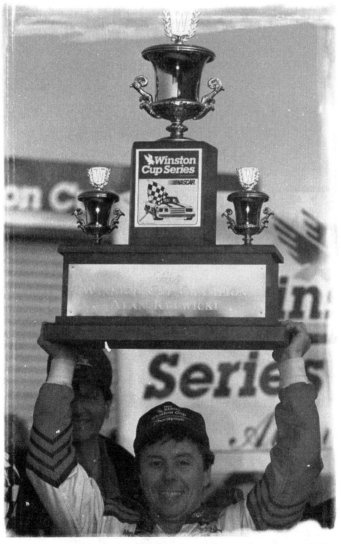

*Alan Kulwicki, after winning Winston
Cup Championship, 11-15-92*

There's a gap in NASCAR's history that will never be filled. One thing many of the sport's greatest stars have shared in their careers is longevity. A racer can compete from his early twenties on into his mid- to late-forties—and even longer for a select few.

But then there are those whose careers are cut short by tragedy.

Tim Richmond, who died of AIDS in 1989, was on the brink of becoming a breakout star with Hendrick Motorsports.

Alan Kulwicki had won the 1992 Cup championship in improbable fashion, driving for a team he owned himself, but in early 1993 he died in a plane crash. And Davey Allison, the son of champion driver Bobby Allison, had already become one of the sport's most popular young stars when he was killed in the crash of a helicopter he was piloting, also in 1993.

Their deaths were tragic, as were the deaths of great drivers like Joe Weatherly, Fireball Roberts, and Dale Earnhardt. Those three, though, were around long enough that fans got to see just how great they really were. With Richmond, Kulwicki, and Allison, however, the story is how so much seemed to still be ahead of them.

Here, we offer a story about each of these drivers that speaks more about how they lived than how they died. The sport will always miss them.

More Than One Way to Skin a Cat

Rick Hendrick's career as a Winston Cup team owner got off to
an interesting start.

Hendrick had owned speedboat racing teams, but got out of
that sport when a driver of one of his boats was killed in an
accident. Hendrick was looking for a place to store his boats
when he learned about Harry Hyde, a former crew chief who'd
had great success with former champion Bobby Isaac but had
fallen out of favor in the NASCAR garage.

Hyde was looking for one more chance to succeed at the
sport's top level, and he saw Hendrick as a ticket to get it.
Hendrick was on his way to becoming one of America's top
automobile dealers, and he'd grown up interested in racing.
Despite the lingering pain from the tragedy with his boat team,
he wasn't a hard sell for Hyde.

In 1983 Hendrick had decided to give NASCAR a try. He
was working on a deal that would have given him Richard
Petty as his driver and country music star Kenny Rogers as a
co-owner.

"We were going to have the king of stock car racing [Petty]
and the king of country music," Hendrick said of the team, which
was called All-Star Racing.

But, as sometimes happens with big deals, things fell apart
when it came down to the details. Hendrick wound up going to
the 1984 Daytona 500 with Geoffrey Bodine, whose back-
ground was in the NASCAR modified series in the Northeast,
as his driver and no sponsor to help him pay the bills. But
Bodine won at Martinsville early in that first season, and All-
Star Racing found its footing. By the end of the team's second
season, the newly named Hendrick Motorsports had picked up

a second sponsor, and Hendrick hired Tim Richmond to drive that car.

He'd also hired Gary Nelson to be a crew chief, but decided that Nelson and Bodine would be a better fit. That left Hyde to run the new team with Richmond. Putting together a grizzled veteran crew chief with a flashy, cocky young driver whose reputation as a party-loving, skirt-chaser gave Hendrick's sponsors some concern.

One of the first appearances Richmond was scheduled to make for the sponsor, Folgers Coffee, was in New Orleans. Richmond arrived the night before and met up with a couple of girls in an airport bar. He took them to his hotel, but they slipped him a "mickey" and took his money and watch.

The next morning, at the appearance, everybody was there except Richmond. Someone was dispatched to the hotel, and Richmond was roused from his artificially deepened sleep. He dressed and hurried to the Folgers appearance but quickly minimized the damage with some self-deprecating humor. "If Folgers can get me up to get here this early, you know it's good," he said.

As many people expected, however, Richmond and Hyde didn't get along well from the start. Hyde believed Richmond didn't know how to drive within the limits of control, while Richmond thought Hyde couldn't build him a car good enough to match his driving talents.

Three things happened to turn things around.

First, Hendrick played some head games with his veteran crew chief. Nelson and Bodine both had innovative minds, and both had started putting some things on their team's cars that Hendrick thought might work for Hyde and Richmond, too.

One night, Hendrick had Nelson go home early, and he brought Hyde over to Bodine's shop. He showed Hyde some of the things Nelson was doing to the cars, but Hyde ridiculed or dismissed it all. It would never work, Hyde huffed.

But, Hendrick said, over the next few races at least some of the stuff Hyde had seen that night wound up showing up in Richmond's cars.

The second thing that helped clear the air was an argument that took place in the trailer Hyde used as his office. Richmond and Hyde started at each other, and Richmond finally told Hyde that if he stepped outside the trailer, he'd whip Hyde's tail. Hyde got up and headed for the door, ready to go.

Richmond, however, started laughing. That just made Hyde angrier. But Richmond was beyond fighting. He'd figured out that no matter what happened, he couldn't win a fight with a man more than twice his age. If he'd won the fight, he was picking on an old man. If he lost the fight, he'd had his tail whipped by an old man. Either way, not good.

That incident, though, seemed to break the ice. Not long after that, the team went to North Wilkesboro Speedway in North Carolina, and Hyde figured out a way to show Richmond something he'd been trying to tell him. He had Richmond make a 50-lap run the way Richmond was used to driving the car. Then, he asked Richmond to run 50 laps the way Hyde wanted him to run—backing off a little earlier going into the turns and trying to take care of the tires.

After 50 laps each way, the tires from Richmond's run were a smoking mess. The tires off the run from Hyde's approach still had some good laps in them. And, on the stopwatch, Hyde's way had been quicker.

Richmond finally got it. From that point on, he and Hyde became the story of the 1986 season. Richmond won six races that summer. —D.P.

Radar Love

Over the past 10 to 15 years, more and more NASCAR drivers, owners, and crew chiefs have acquired motor homes that allow them to stay right at the race track instead of fighting the traffic coming in and leaving the track each day.

It's become quite the "arms race," frankly, with each person seemingly trying to find the bus with the most high-tech gizmos and the most expensive toys. Satellite dishes, allowing the NASCAR glitterati access to hundreds of channels for their plasma-screen televisions, are a must. Speed Channel, undoubtedly, has pretty good ratings in the motor home park. Racers love to watch other racers compete.

But another channel that's big in the motor homes is The Weather Channel. Weather is important to racing, not only because rain means no practice or no qualifying or no race, but because engines and cars behave differently in cold weather than in heat or when it's cloudy or sunny. Several drivers are pilots, too, and pilots need to have a certain fascination with weather to help keep them flying.

It's easy to forget, though, that everybody in racing wasn't always a meteorologist. Just ask Larry McReynolds.

McReynolds, who has been an analyst for FOX Sports' NASCAR broadcasts since 2001, enjoyed a long, successful career as a crew chief. In 1992 he was working at Robert

Yates Racing as crew chief on the No. 28 Fords driven by Davey Allison.

The '92 season had been remarkable, in good ways and bad ones, for McReynolds and Allison. They'd won the Daytona 500, for starters, but in April his grandfather, Edmund Jacob "Pop" Allison, died.

Allison then won the Winston 500 at Talladega, giving him victories in the first two of the four races that made up the "Winston Million," a bonus plan from R.J. Reynolds Tobacco that paid a $1 million bonus to any driver who could win three of those races—the Daytona 500, the Winston 500, the Coca-Cola 600 at Charlotte, and the Southern 500 at Darlington.

Before Allison could worry about trying to win the $1 million at Charlotte in May, he competed in the first all-star race held under the track's new lights. It was promoted as "One Hot Night," and it lived up to that billing.

Allison had won the all-star race the previous year and started on the pole in 1992. By late in the final segment, which is where the $200,000 first prize was paid, he was third behind Kyle Petty and Dale Earnhardt.

On the final lap, Petty and Earnhardt made contact in Turn 3 as they fought for the lead. Earnhardt spun and was out of contention, but because Petty had to slow so dramatically to keep from wrecking, too, Allison caught up, and Petty began trying to block him off the final turn. They were side-by-side coming to the finish line, with Allison a nose ahead just as they took the checkered flag. Their cars made contact, and Allison piled into the wall, driver's side first.

Allison had been knocked out momentarily, but he came to about the time McReynolds got to his car.

"I knew he wasn't hurt-hurt," McReynolds said. "But I knew he was knocked kind of coo-coo."

McReynolds watched the emergency workers cut Allison from the car, but he also kept one eye on the scoreboard. He wanted to see what car number wound up at the top when NASCAR officials finished reviewing the finish.

"It seemed like it took about two hours, and it was probably two minutes," McReynolds said. "Finally, they flipped that No. 28 up top. It was like, 'Yes!'"

Allison had a concussion and several other injuries. Instead of going to victory lane, he got a ride in an ambulance to the infield care center and, later, to a local hospital.

"What happened?" Allison said to McReynolds as they rode toward the infield care center.

"You won the race, Davey," McReynolds said.

"You're shittin' me," Allison said.

"No, Davey, you won the race," McReynolds repeated.

"You're not shittin' me?" Allison asked again.

"Davey, I wouldn't shit you about something like that," McReynolds said. "You won the race."

Earnhardt came back the next week to win the 600, though, denying Allison his first shot at the Winston Million.

Later that summer, Allison was one of the drivers taking part in a "tire test" at Indianapolis Motor Speedway, the first time stock cars had ever been there and a precursor to the Brickyard 400 that would begin in 1994.

In July at Pocono, Allison's car was strong, but a mistake on a pit stop had him back in traffic. As he tried to come back to the front, though, on lap 150 he went into Turn 2—the same turn where his father, Bobby, has suffered career-ending injuries in a crash four years earlier—and got hit by Darrell Waltrip.

Allison's car turned sideways and went into the grass, then flipped backward and began a violent series of 11 barrel rolls. Amazingly, Allison survived. He was beaten and bruised and spent the next week in the hospital. He flew back to Alabama on Friday, determined to be in his car for the start of the next race at Talladega so he'd get the points and stay in the championship battle.

Allison had suffered a broken right wrist in the crash at Pocono. "We had to put Velcro on the palm of his racing glove pulled over his cast and on the shifter," McReynolds said. "The only way he could shift was to have his hand Velcroed to the shifter." That helped him get to the first yellow flag in the race on Sunday.

The next month at Michigan, Allison's brother, Clifford, wrecked during a Busch Series practice session and was killed.

So by the time Allison, McReynolds, and their team got to Darlington for the Southern 500 on Labor Day weekend, they'd already been through a lot. Now, they had a chance to become the first team since Bill Elliott's in 1985 to win the $1 million bonus.

When Elliott had won the $1 million in 1985, the number on the roof of his car had been accidentally affixed upside down. McReynolds had the No. 28 affixed to Allison's Ford that same way this time, trying to think of everything possible to help his driver.

Allison had been in contention all day, and as the final 100 miles of the Southern 500 approached, McReynolds faced a crucial decision. The No. 28 Ford needed fuel, but bad weather was threatening, and if rain was going to cut the race short, Allison needed to stay out as long as he could.

McReynolds motioned one of his team's members over to him and hollered toward him over the pit road din.

"Go check the radar," he ordered.

The team member ran off toward the NASCAR truck, which had a weather radar monitor. A few more laps, and a few more gulps of fuel, passed before his return.

"It looks good," the team member said.

Thus advised, McReynolds ordered Allison to come to pit road for enough fuel to go the full 500-mile distance.

A few laps later, the rain started.

It didn't last long, but it had rained enough and it was getting late enough in the day that NASCAR chose not to restart the race. Waltrip, who hadn't pitted, was declared the winner.

McReynolds, of course, was confused. He found his weather messenger and asked for an explanation. The crew member could not understand what went wrong. He'd gone to the truck and looked at the radar.

"There was green everywhere around us," he told McReynolds.

In racing, of course, green means go. On that radar, though, it had meant rain. If only McReynolds' messenger had known that.—D.P.

Ol' Blue Eyes

Alan Kulwicki went into the final race of the 1992 just 30 points behind Davey Allison in the race for the Winston Cup title.

Bill Elliott was just 10 points behind Kulwicki, and there were also three other drivers mathematically eligible to win the championship after the Hooters 500 at Atlanta Motor Speedway.

NASCAR had never seen anything like this championship battle. And it wasn't like there wasn't anything else to talk about going into that race, either. It was going to be the last race that Richard Petty, the sport's all-time winningest driver, competed in. The sport had spent the entire season saying good-bye to its "King," but the final weekend was going to be special. Petty was going to be the focus of all sorts of activities and ceremonies, including a big party televised on national cable TV on the night before the race.

With the championship race so close, however, there was almost too much going on for everyone to digest. It wouldn't be until several years later that the significance of the fact that the Hooters 500 was also Jeff Gordon's first career Cup race could be fully appreciated.

Elliott had been well ahead in the standings with just six races left in the season, and Kulwicki dropped so far behind even he felt like his chances to win a title had slipped away. After a wreck at Dover, he was 278 points behind and all but convinced it was over.

But Kulwicki hadn't made it to where he was giving up. He'd run almost an entire season with just one race car after moving to North Carolina from Wisconsin to go racing. He'd also turned away from a chance to join car owner Junior Johnson's super team, in large part because he just didn't think he could do things the way he wanted to do them if he was driving another man's cars.

As the principle players began to gather in Atlanta for that race, Kulwicki had been cajoled by his public relations man, Tom Roberts, to come to town a day early to do interviews with newspaper, radio, and television outlets in the Atlanta area. It had taken some doing, since Kulwicki felt he needed to be doing last-minute work on his No. 7 Ford instead.

At lunch on that day, Kulwicki and Roberts were going into a Hooters restaurant for a press conference with newspaper writers. Hooters was not only sponsoring the season's final race, but it was also the primary sponsor on Kulwicki's car.

On their way to that lunch-time gathering, Roberts asked Kulwicki a question he'd been needing to ask for days. ESPN, which would be covering the championship banquet at season's end, was planning to put highlights of the champion's year over music for the show, and they'd asked each driver to pick a song he thought might be appropriate. Roberts asked Kulwicki what song he'd like to hear, but Kulwicki gave Roberts no answer. That didn't bother Roberts, since he knew the driver sometimes thought a long time about what he wanted to say.

The luncheon and the rest of the day's activities went well, and that night as Roberts and Kulwicki returned to the hotel where they'd started their day, Kulwicki was about to get out and go inside when he stopped and finally answered Roberts' question.

So after Kulwicki had finished second to Elliott in the Hooters 500 on that Sunday, but had stretched his fuel long enough so that he led the most laps and got five bonus points for doing so, Kulwicki won the championship by a mere 10 points.

And when the time came in December for Kulwicki to come to the stage in New York's Waldorf-Astoria Hotel to accept the champion's awards, the music that played was the only song that really ever should have been considered.

When he was getting out of the car on that night in Atlanta, Kulwicki had turned to Roberts and said, "My Way."

It had been hours since Roberts had asked the question. For a minute, he was confused.

"Huh?" Roberts said.

"The song," Kulwicki said. "For the banquet. 'My Way.'"

"Oh," Roberts said, with the light going on in his head. "Okay."

"Yes," Kulwicki said. "'My Way.' But the Frank Sinatra version. It has to be Sinatra." —D.P.

chapter 11
No. 3,
but One of a Kind

*Dale Earnhardt and Junior
before Rolex 24 Hours of Daytona*

In many ways Dale Earnhardt's life and career is the very embodiment of stock-car racing.

He grew up watching his father, Ralph, drive on dirt tracks across the Southeast, making a living by battling fender to fender for lap after lap, trying to keep food on the table.

Earnhardt scratched and clawed his way into the sport, too, borrowing money on Fridays to buy tires to race with on Saturday night, knowing that if he didn't win enough money he couldn't pay back the money he'd borrowed.

He won rookie of the year honors in 1979 and, the next year, won a Winston Cup championship. From the time he and team owner Richard Childress hooked up for good in 1984 and started running the No. 3 car, Earnhardt's legend just kept growing.

To start looking back at Earnhardt's career, we begin with a story Jim McLaurin wrote for *The State* in Columbia, South Carolina, on November 13, 1994, after Earnhardt won his seventh Cup title.

The Fast Lane: Earnhardt Finds Fame a Constant Burden

There is something robot-like in Dale Earnhardt as he goes about his life as the world's greatest race car driver.

It is almost as if he is a great Shakespearean actor, delivering Hamlet's soliloquy with such apparent fervor that women in the audience swoon and grown men reach for their handkerchiefs—all the while thinking, "If I don't get out of these tights soon, I'm going to pass out."

Whether it's signing autographs even as he's carrying on a conversation with someone else, or walking within a phalanx of security guards while his adoring fans reach out just to touch him, something in Earnhardt's demeanor tells you that sometimes his mind and his body are not in the same place.

Even in moments of joy, there is a part of the man that he keeps to one corner of a private little room within himself. No one is invited in.

But, sometimes, the door opens just a crack.

Earnhardt was enjoying the post-race, post-championship banter with the press after his win in the ACDelco 500 in Rockingham—which also locked up his seventh Winston Cup championship—saying all the right things, getting the appropriate laughs, when the question came from out of the blue:

"Dale," a reporter asked, "after the accident in February, did you ever feel like you might not be emotionally ready to do what you needed to do to win the championship?"

"What?" Earnhardt asked, not quite comprehending the question.

"After Neil Bonnett's accident," the reporter said.

There was a long pause. Earnhardt dropped his head slightly, shielding his eyes under the bill of the ever-present baseball cap.

"I'd rather not elaborate on that," he said, then paused again. When he looked up, there was genuine pain in his face. His voice was halting when he spoke: "I can't go fishing in my own lake because of Neil," he said. "Because we fished in it all the time. I can't….I've tried….It's Neil's pond."

There was a rare silence in the press box. Earnhardt, in a most simple way, had shown us the grief he still carried over the loss of the best friend, to whom he'd dedicated his championship.

In those fleeting moments, we had gotten a peek inside that tiny room. We would not be allowed to stay. Earnhardt gently but firmly closed the door.

"Here," he said, with mock gruffness, reaching over to grab the microphone from the moderator. "It's my championship, ain't it?"—meaning, let's move on.

The expected laugh came.

The tension was broken, and there was an embarrassed relief on both sides; Earnhardt, for having let us inside, and the reporters, for having seen—if only for a flicker—an intensely personal side of a very private man.

There is an almost mystical aura about Earnhardt, that somehow the racing gods reached down and endowed him at birth with superhuman qualities; that he just "happened."

But that's not so. His only gift, if you can call it that, was being born in the right place at the right time.

"I could rattle 'em off," he said. "From Ned Jarrett to Tiny Lund to Humpy Wheeler to Richard Howard—the Pearsons,

the Pettys, the Yarboroughs—everybody has made me a
better racer.

"People say I'm from the old school: 'He's aggressive. He
races harder than he should sometimes.' But I learned from the
guys who raced like that."

If there's one thing Earnhardt understands, it's where
he came from, and the people who helped him get to where
he is.

"I tell you," Earnhardt said, "I've been fortunate to, one, have
had a great life as a kid growing up around a racing family and
a dad that raced, and then having great friends in racing that
helped me along when I started racing.

"Guys from Richard Petty on down have helped me. The
Allisons, David Pearson, everybody. Tiny Lund, I had some great
sportsman races with him at Hickory Speedway and places like
that. Bobby Isaac…I could name guys that got me going in this
sport, and it's carried me to where I am today. I've learned from
the best. I learned from the legends."

There's no insincerity, then, when Earnhardt says he will
never replace Petty as the king of stock car racing, nor false
humility.

Petty, Earnhardt says, has done things for the sport that no
man ever has nor ever will. Not just the 200 victories that will
likely never be surpassed, nor the seven championships, which
Earnhardt has equaled.

Petty made racing respectable, and racers respected.

"I just tried to put it out of my mind of tying Richard Petty's
record," Earnhardt said. "I knew what it would mean. It would
mean a lot to me, and I'm proud and honored to be in the same
group, as far as being tied with him.

"But he's still the king. He's done it all. He pioneered it and got us to where we are today. I can't take that away from him; I don't care how much I win or what I do."

Dale Earnhardt lives in a world of big money, fast cars, and life-in-the-balance decisions made in the blink of an eye. It is a world of smoke and noise and danger and bravery and sometimes tragedy.

His skill has made him wealthy beyond his wildest dreams, and an object of the kind of adulation that must seem strange to a simple man who grew up with no other ambition than to drive a race car.

It is a world that makes big heroes. And right now, love him or hate him, Earnhardt is the biggest.

But fame carries a heavy price. He is tugged at constantly from all directions; an autograph here, a public appearance there, a sponsorship commitment halfway across the country—all at the same time.

"I tell you," he said, "it beats you down, with all the ways people pull on you for time or whatever it may be. It's all part of the game, and it's gotten more and bigger and bigger."

Earnhardt is not comfortable being an idol. In one breath he says that he loves his fans, and he's sincere. In the next, the constant adulation is "a big part of my life that I don't really enjoy, but you've just got to smile and say yes or okay or sign that autograph or whatever."

Time is a racer's most important commodity, whether it's the thousandths of a second he can shave off of a lap, or the few hours he can get away from the clamor. Of the latter, he says, there is precious little.

"It's unbelievable," he said. "If you could follow me around for a day, it would probably amaze you.

"Sometimes about 3:00 in the afternoon I'm about ready to blow my brains out. On a Tuesday or a Wednesday, when you're trying to straighten out everything that's going on and where you're going and what's happening.

"I sign autographs, on average, an hour and a half every day in the office, and I'm still a week behind, and it's piling up. The fan response is great. That's the part you do and love; everything's part of the job.

"I've learned a lot about it, though. I'm learning every day how to handle it. I wasn't too good at it in '79 and '80, but I've learned to smile a little bit."

On the Wednesday before the ACDelco 500, Earnhardt had finished a press conference and stood in a small hallway chatting with a few friends. Perhaps unwittingly, he said something that goes a long way in explaining why, at times, he seems to be on remote control.

"I make a lot of phone calls that nobody knows about," Earnhardt said. "To sick people; to kids who are dying.

"I called the preacher the other day and asked him to come out to the farm. We rode off over on a back corner and had a long talk. I asked him, 'What do you say to people like that? How do you handle it?'...

"I can send them autographed caps or pictures or call them on the phone," he said. "But sometimes people want things out of Dale Earnhardt that he just can't deliver." —J.M.

A "Goll-eee" Moment

It is difficult for race fans today to think of Dale Earnhardt in any other terms than as "the Intimidator."

But there was a time when Earnhardt was young and impressionable, and nowhere was that more evident than when he and his buddies went to Daytona to race for the first time in 1976.

Earnhardt and his brothers Danny and Randy, along with long-time crew chief and lifelong friend Tony Eury, Rick Bost, and Mike Bostick, who would later become Earnhardt's brother-in-law, loaded his late-model sportsman race car and all packed into an old beat-up one-ton Chevy truck and headed for the beach.

"It was my dad's truck, and we put a case of oil on the back when we left home," Earnhardt recalled in an interview in 1998. "When we got back, we didn't have a can left. Every time we'd stop for gas, we'd put in two quarts of oil. She was a pretty wore-out truck."

Earnhardt said that his first impression of the track as they exited I-95 onto Volusia Boulevard in Daytona was not intimidated, but even he had to gulp.

"We saw the end of the race track and kept driving by, kept driving by, and I said, 'Oh Lord, how big is this thing?'" he said. "You see pictures of it, and see it on TV, but you never realize how big this place is. That was a pretty awesome deal right there, driving by the place, then the next morning when we went in for inspection, and it was unbelievable."

Earnhardt qualified 22nd for his first race at Daytona and, he said, "finished 13th with bad fuel filter. Should have been better."

But there was nothing like the experience.

"I never remember being scared of what was going on," Earnhardt said. "It was like the whole time was unbelievable, and we were just having a big time the whole time.

"I'd be walking around and there would go Richard Petty, and here would go David Pearson. What time I wasn't on the track, I was watching them, watching around the Winston Cup garage. It was something else."

But, even then, he had a little bit of the Intimidator in him.

"Turn off your tape recorder," he said, "and I'll tell you about the night life." —J.M.

Over? Who Says It's Over?

At times, it looked as if Dale Earnhardt was inventing new ways to lose the Daytona 500. But in none of those races that he lost did he get a bigger roar out of the crowd than in 1997.

Earnhardt and his nemesis, Jeff Gordon, were battling for second place while chasing down leader Bill Elliott with 11 laps to go when they came off the second turn side-by-side.

Earnhardt's car carried to the outside wall, and when he bounced off it, he tagged Gordon, then got hit from behind by Dale Jarrett. His black GM Goodwrench Chevrolet went back into the wall and flipped onto its roof, then slid down the backstretch before it flipped onto its wheels in the grass.

The fans in the frontstretch who had seen the tumble on the giant TV screen could not believe what they saw next. Even as the caution flag was still flying, Earnhardt came tearing around the Turn 4 apron in the badly damaged car, setting off a roar that drowned out the engines of the race cars.

After Earnhardt had climbed out of the car, he walked to the ambulance and then walked back to the wreck, which was being hooked to the tow truck.

"I looked at the wheels and told the guy in the car to fire it up," Earnhardt said. "It fired up and I said, 'Get out! Unhook me! I've got to go!'"

His dream of winning the big one was on hold for another year, but Earnhardt didn't cast any blame on Gordon.

"After it was all over," Gordon said, "I saw this mangled black No. 3 car coming and I said, 'Uh-oh.' But he came by and gave me a thumbs up. To me, that was an okay, that he wasn't putting any blame on my side."

Earnhardt and his crew's heroic efforts to pound his car into good enough shape to finish the race turned out to be largely symbolic because he would have dropped only one spot in the finishing order. But the fact that they did said a lot about why—and how—Earnhardt won seven Winston Cup titles.

"We took off after 'em," Earnhardt said. "You've got to get every lap you can. That's what we're running for the championship for." —J.M.

A Sure Thing for a Dream

What would make a man who has reached the top of his profession chuck it all to pursue a dream? For Kirk Shelmerdine, the dream was reason enough.

Shelmerdine, who went South from Pennsylvania in 1981 to chase his dream to be a Winston Cup driver, saw his road take a detour (almost) when he passed the Mason-Dixon Line. Instead of becoming a driver, he became one of the most successful mechanics the sport of auto racing had ever seen.

"When I was a teenager and moved down here, I wanted to be a driver," Shelmerdine said. "That was my motivation for getting into racing. I always had that kind of desire in me. I was wired for it. But the opportunities never represented themselves in such a way that that was my best move to do so.

"I got involved in the mechanical end, and that lasted an awful long time. I saw an awful lot of success there."

Success indeed.

After two years of being a one-man crew for independent driver James Hylton, Shelmerdine signed on with a young owner-driver named Richard Childress and in doing so, hitched his wagon to a star.

Childress re-signed a driver he couldn't afford a couple of years earlier, and the threesome made history. Dale Earnhardt became the most successful driver of the 1980s and 1990s, winning six of his seven championships from 1986 to 1994, and Shelmerdine was the man under the hood for four of those titles.

As the crew chief on Earnhardt's No. 3 Chevrolets, he became the youngest crew chief to win a Winston Cup race, at 25 in 1983, and at 28, he became the youngest to win a Winston Cup championship. At 29, he was inducted into the International Mechanics Hall of Fame.

Clearly, Shelmerdine was cut from special cloth, and the combination of Earnhardt, Childress, and himself could have won more titles. (Earnhardt won his sixth and seventh in 1993 and 1994, after Shelmerdine left.) In fact, had he stayed, they probably would have broken Earnhardt's and Richard Petty's shared record of seven championships.

But as good as he was at it, being a mechanic was, in the end, just a job. Driving a race car, the dream he'd put on hold in 1981, was his passion.

So with the world on a string, he cut that string, said good-bye to the big money, and basically started over. He opened his own little shop in Welcome, North Carolina, right down the street from Childress.

With an annual budget that would not have covered the expenses of one race with his old team, Shelmerdine would never again enjoy the success he had as a crew chief, but he found happiness instead.

"Someday I'll put all my 101 reasons in a book," he said, "but for now, I'll say it got old, I guess. I was burned out. Totally.

"It wasn't one main straw that broke the camel's back; it was a combination of things. I put all the pros and cons together and presented them to myself in a clear way, and the cons clearly outweighed the pros. I had to go. There was no use to try to Band-Aid it or go ask the boss for more money or look for some other reason to do it. If you're not happy and not able to give 100 percent, you shouldn't be doing it."

Shelmerdine loved the driving but couldn't pay the bills, so he hired himself out as a "consultant" from time to time, and even had offers from team owners to be a combination driver–crew chief, but he was not so dumb that he couldn't see that all they wanted was his mechanical skills, not his driving ones.

"In 1994 and '95, I took a Busch (Series) ride that was supposed to be full-time, with sponsorship and stuff, and the second time I even came up with the sponsorship," he said. "I went to the car owner, he took all the money, bought a new tractor-trailer, and fired me after the first seven races....I wanted the driving thing to blossom into something probably a little bit too badly."

He has enjoyed what could generously be called "modest success" as a driver, racing in minor league circuits all over the country, and by 2005 he had worked himself into a position where he was making a full-time attempt at the Nextel Cup circuit, though without much success.

He may one day change his mind and take a crew chief's job again, but it would not be because it's what he wants. Even if another wealthy team owner such as Rick Hendrick came along and offered him the moon, he'd be hard-pressed to take it.

"In the first place, he wouldn't do that," Shelmerdine said. "Second, I don't know if I could actually justify it. What have I got to gain? I've already won enough of those [championship] belt buckles to last a while. Forty-six races. What is there for me to shoot at? Driving presented that for me. It was kind of a lofty goal that got my enthusiasm going again.

"It is all the same old BS I've been doing for years, but from a whole new perspective.

"Looking through the windshield is different. It presented me a whole new ladder to climb." —J.M.

A Penny for Your Thoughts

When Tony Stewart started climbing fences after winning races during the 2005 season, it was another take on victory celebrations that have always been a part of the story in NASCAR.

Alan Kulwicki, the driver-owner who shocked the stock-car racing world in 1992 by winning the championship, was known for his "Polish victory lap." Kulwicki wanted to see the fans cheering him when he went around the track after a win, so he turned around and went clockwise on an oval with the driver's side toward the grandstands.

The crowd loved it, but NASCAR wasn't so thrilled. Afraid that other cars or track safety vehicles might not be expecting Kulwicki to be coming the "wrong" way, he was "urged" by NASCAR not to make a habit of doing the reverse lap. He promised he wouldn't do it again until he won the Daytona 500 or the championship, so after he finished second in the Hooters 500 at Atlanta Motor Speedway in 1992, edging Bill Elliott for the championship, Kulwicki broke it out again.

Drivers have done various versions of burnouts and doughnuts over the years.

Kyle Busch, after winning a Busch race at Charlotte, spun his tires to create a cloud of smoke and then climbed out of his car so he could be there, standing on the window sill to salute the fans, when the smokescreen dissipated.

Two of the most famous post-race celebrations came after veteran stars got their first Daytona 500 victories after years and years of trying. Darrell Waltrip had failed to win the sport's biggest race in 17 tries, but in 1989 he and crew chief Jeff Hammond saw opportunity present itself. Waltrip stayed on the track and stretched his final load of fuel for more that 130 miles.

And won the Daytona 500.

"This is Daytona isn't it?" Waltrip asked in victory lane. "Don't lie to me! Don't tell me I am dreaming!"

Waltrip then did his version of the "Icky shuffle," mimicking— quite poorly—the end-zone dance done by Cincinnati Bengals football player Icky Woods, "spiking" his driver's helmet in the process.

Nine years later, history would repeat itself when another long-time superstar ended a career filled with Daytona 500 frustration by winning the race in his 20th try.

Earnhardt was leading the final lap in 1990 when he had a flat tire going into Turn 3, and Derrike Cope went by him to win. In 1993 Dale Jarrett had passed Earnhardt in the final laps on his way to winning the 500.

Finally, in 1998, Earnhardt got to the checkers first. He took a long, slow lap around the track and then, as he came off Turn 4 and headed down pit road, crews from virtually every team in the sport were lined up to congratulate him. It was an amazing sight, a tribute to one of NASCAR's all-time best.

When Earnhardt had slapped the last high-five, he gunned the engine of his black No. 3 Chevrolet and looped it twice in the infield grass. It wasn't until later, after the excitement of the moment died down, that people began to realize that the mark Earnhardt had left in the grass looked very much like the number "3." Could he have possibly done that on purpose?

More than an hour after that race, with Earnhardt high above the track in the press box doing the winner's interview he'd always wanted to do, fans began doing the strangest thing.

Carrying their coolers and souvenir bags they'd had with them all day, a few of them went into the infield grass and began picking up chunks of grass from where Earnhardt had made his mark.

There are all kinds of great stories about how Earnhardt celebrated that night. Hours later, ESPN was on the air doing a late *SportsCenter*, and Earnhardt was seen riding past their broadcast position on the back of a security guard's motorcycle. Much, much later, he was down on the beach with some friends toasting the victory with the trophy still in his hands.

At 4:30 PM Sunday afternoon, about an hour after the Daytona 500 ended, the first fan got in line to be one of 180 to be admitted into a question-and-answer session at Daytona USA, which would follow the ceremony where the race-winning car was put on display for a year in the museum. More than two dozen fans spent the night in line, sitting through a driving rain. The line for seats was cut off at 7:30 the next morning.

"Race fans are pretty special people," Earnhardt said. "I have signed autographs where people have had to stand in line out in the rain and they said, 'I wouldn't have stood in line for Elvis, but I stood in line for you.'"

It was at that Monday morning ceremony when Earnhardt told reporters about a little girl he'd met on the day before his big victory. She was one of five children from the Make-A-Wish Foundation that Earnhardt met on that Saturday.

"She was rubbing this penny, a brand new one, and she gave it to me," Earnhardt said. "She said, 'I've rubbed this penny and it's going to help you win the Daytona 500. It's your race.'"

The next day, Earnhardt glued the penny to the dashboard of his car. And for the next year, that penny stayed glued to that dashboard there at Daytona USA.

"For a little girl like that in a wheelchair, who life hasn't been so good to, for her to give me a penny for good luck in the Daytona 500, that's pretty special," Earnhardt said.

It certainly was. —D.P.

chapter 12
Modern-Day Heroes

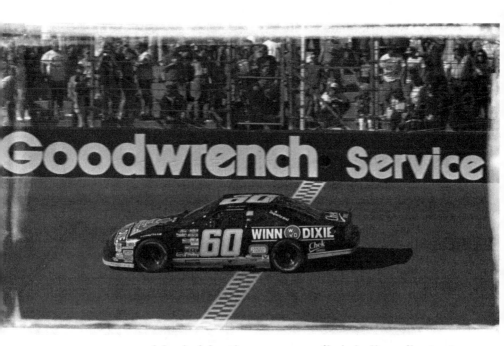

Mark Martin crosses finish line first at North Carolina Motor Speedway to win Goodwrench 200, 2-24-96

Sometimes it seems people only tell stories about the guys who're no longer racing. But some of the guys who're still around have had their moments, too.

Unanswered Prayers

In 1995, Dale Jarrett figured his time with Robert Yates Racing was done.

He'd come to the team after Ernie Irvan was seriously injured in a crash a year earlier at Michigan International Speedway, but Irvan had made a miraculous recovery and was nearly ready to return.

That August, Jarrett and his wife, Kelley, were riding in a car with Yates in Indianapolis when Yates said he didn't know if he could make a two-car team work. Jarrett was not surprised by his car owner's position. Multicar teams were not nearly as prevalent in the sport then as they are today. Jarrett knew that it was likely he'd need to have another option when it was time for Irvan to come back.

Jarrett had a sponsor lined up with which he could start his own team. The sponsor had offered more money that Jarrett thought he needed to get a team started. But there was a problem.

Jarrett was a husband and a father—with daughters ages 7 and 5 at the time—and the potential sponsor was Hooters Restaurants, not a particularly good fit.

"Even though it's a very good company, it wouldn't have exactly fit the image that I was trying to portray," Jarrett said. "Making appearances at Hooters wasn't exactly what I wanted to do, and it certainly wasn't what Kelley Jarrett wanted Dale to be doing. But she understood what we had to do. We had to worry about my family and making a living and getting something started."

The contract was on Jarrett's desk, needing only his signature. But Jarrett waited. Several weeks later, Yates decided that he would, indeed, start a second team.

"I realized then and there that's why I hadn't signed that contract," Jarrett said. "There was going to be something there waiting for me. Everybody says God works in mysterious ways. You just don't know. Good things come to those to wait. I waited, and look what happened."

What happened was the No. 88 Ford, the car Jarrett drove to victories in the 1996 Daytona 500, Coca-Cola 600, and Brickyard 400, all within a year of thinking his days with Yates were done. He went on to win the 1999 championship and is still driving that No. 88 Ford. —D.P.

Walk Softly, but Keep the Stick Handy

Two-time NASCAR Winston Cup champion Terry Labonte is one of the quietest and most unassuming men in racing, but his calm exterior hides a fierce competitor inside.

When Labonte won the 1995 Goody's 500 at Bristol, he did it by surviving a crash initiated by seven-time champion Dale Earnhardt at the checkered flag. Labonte didn't raise a big stink, but if it had gone the other way it could have been a different story.

"I won the race, so I'm not mad," Labonte said afterward. "If he had won the race, I might be a little mad. But I don't think he intended to wreck us. We were just both trying to win the race."

But fellow competitor Bobby Hamilton recalled an incident when Labonte was not as forgiving.

"I remember the time that Lake Speed spun Terry out at Bristol," Hamilton said. "They worked on that car and worked on that car. Terry didn't say nothing to nobody. Terry goes back out, wrecks it, pulls back in, and leaves. Terry has a reputation. When you get to Terry, you'd better pass him in a racing-like manner or you're going to get it back. Everybody knows that."

Except maybe one man.

In the 1999 version of the same race at Bristol, Earnhardt did his damage a little earlier, knocking Labonte out of the way on the backstretch on the final lap, going on to take the checkered flag. Earnhardt semi-apologized, saying he only meant to "rattle his cage a little bit," but Labonte came back across his bow with a warning: "He'd better tighten his belts up." —J.M.

Two Sides of the Coin

Ricky Craven has seen both sides of what racing can bring.

He worked his way up through the NASCAR ranks and got a ride with Hendrick Motorsports, one of the most accomplished teams in the Cup Series. But after finishing third in the 1997 Daytona 500 and fifth in the next race at Rockingham, Craven suffered a concussion, a broken shoulder blade, and two broken ribs in a crash at Texas Motor Speedway. He missed two races but returned to run the rest of that season in the No. 25 Chevrolets.

Just four races into the 1998 season, however, Craven admitted that he wasn't 100 percent. He was experiencing headaches and dizziness, and after tests at a hospital he was diagnosed with post-concussion syndrome. He ran four more races for Hendrick Motorsports after returning later that year, but lost the ride he'd worked his whole life to get.

Craven spent the next two seasons trying to convince the garage area that he'd fully recovered. He drove for under-funded teams and did wonders just to get his car into the field most weeks. There were times when he doubted himself, wondered if he'd ever get back in a competitive race car.

But he never gave up.

Late in the 2000 season, as he was trying to convince car owner Cal Wells to let him drive his cars the following year, Craven and his sister, Lauri, opened a store to sell snowmobiles, motorcycles, and all-terrain vehicles in the coastal town of Belfast, Maine, a half-hour's drive from their hometown of Newburgh. The store was across the road from a restaurant where the family used to sit around and eat lobsters on those New England summer evenings that make winter there worth enduring.

Craven knew how much his success in racing meant to the people in that region. So he put up the trophies he'd won in the Busch North and Busch Series and the pictures of him with Jeff Gordon and Dale Earnhardt.

Just more than a year later, Craven was able to put another trophy on display in Maine for his fans to see. In the 30th race of the 2001 season, driving the No. 32 Chevrolet owned by Wells, Craven outdueled Dale Jarrett in the final laps to get his first Cup victory at Martinsville Speedway.

Then, in March 2003, Craven and Kurt Busch banged sheet metal all the way down the frontstretch on the final lap of the Dodge 400 at Darlington Raceway. In one of the closest—and best—races in NASCAR history, Craven was ahead at the checkered flag by just two one-thousandths of a second. There has never been a closer finish since NASCAR began using electronic scoring.

When the Cup circuit returned to Darlington later that year for the Southern 500, everybody wanted to talk to Craven about his incredible victory less than six months earlier.

Just after 9:00 AM on race day, only hours before he'd climb back in the car at the track where he'd had the most rewarding moment of his career, the telephone rang in his motor home.

"It's gone," Lauri said, through tears. "It's just gone."

Firemen would eventually surmise that the fire had started near some electrical boxes at the center of the Cravens' store in Belfast, Maine. When the first fire trucks arrived, the fire was already raging. Holes were cut in the roof to vent the intense heat. Lauri arrived and wanted to go inside, hoping she could save something, but firefighters held her back. More volunteer companies showed up to help. Someone knocked in the front door, and the blaze got a fresh gulp of oxygen and flared.

A forklift had been pulled inside for the weekend, and the fire got to it. When its propane fuel tank exploded, the firemen could only pour water to keep the blaze from spreading and had to let the fire burn itself out.

Craven finished eighth in the Southern 500. He honored a commitment to sign autographs at a track in Greenville, South Carolina, the next night. On Tuesday, he went to Maine to see what was left of the place that had been so much more than a family business. It was a place Craven visited often, where he saw his fans and signed autographs and rekindled the strong bond the driver had with those who'd supported him.

Craven didn't get there until around 11:30 PM.

"The very front part of the building was there," he said. "The windows and doors were gone, but I took a flashlight and pointed it in. You couldn't see anything, because there was nothing for the light to reflect off of. It was just black. Imagine a campfire that has burned out. That's what it looked like."

Craven thought it might look better the next morning. There had to be something worth saving. Anything. A trophy, a photograph. Something, But Lauri had been right. It was gone. It was just gone.

Just inside the front door, however, Craven saw something.

It was a coin, a medallion from a box containing one of the No. 32 die-cast cars Craven's fans could buy at the shop. The car was on one side and Craven's signature was on the other.

Somehow, it had survived.

Craven was let go from his Cup ride late in the 2004 season. He drove for Roush Racing in the Craftsman Truck Series in 2005, but the promise that team showed early in the year never played out.

"It takes every ounce of your effort when you're not running well, it just seems like everything is so much harder," Craven said. "But there will be a day when I can think back about having won at every level I've raced and persevering through a lot of stuff."

Craven has kept that coin that survived the fire in 2003. Sometimes he takes it out, looks at it, and wonders why it made it through...and why he found it.

"Some days I look at it and know there are some memories caught up in it," Craven says. "Some days, though, I almost want to get rid of it. People might think it would be a prized possession, but in reality it's almost the reverse of that. I really don't know quite why I've got it or what it represents."

In one regard, though, nothing could be more appropriate.

Trophies remind you of the good times, the days when things lined up and racing seemed easy. Days like March 16, 2003, when Craven barely beat Busch to the finish line in one of the most memorable finishes in NASCAR history.

But nobody knows better than Craven that the bad days—when you shine your light and see only blackness, when things seemingly have been reduced to only a pile of ashes—are ultimately what makes the good ones seem so much better.

The happy times and the hard ones.

Highlights and heartbreaks.

Two sides to a coin. —D.P.

Not Too Cool for School

Mark Martin grew up in Batesville, Arkansas, and today he's one of that town's most famous citizens.

He's got a Ford dealership in town now, and he has built a museum there housing as much of the memorabilia from his incredible racing career as he's been able to get his hands on.

Martin has had a lot of great memories in NASCAR. When he won at Kansas Speedway in 2005, it gave him 35 career Nextel Cup victories to go with an all-time record 47 wins in the Busch Series. He also won a sixth career championship in the International Race of Champions Series, the 11th straight time that he's entered that series in which he's finished either first or second.

He's certainly come a long, long way from how things were when he started racing through life in Batesville.

"When I was in high school in Batesville, I felt like I was treated like a strange weirdo," Martin says. "I couldn't play sports—the kind of sports you play in high school—very well. But once I found out that I could race those cars, I knew that's what I wanted to do."

Martin remembers winning the national short track championship race in Rockford, Illinois, in 1977.

"That was one of the most significant victories of my career, and I was still in high school when I won it," Martin recalls. "I qualified second. Dick Trickle had fast time that day. We did not have the first clue what we were doing and we won the race. It was huge. I still have pictures. I mean, this was a really big deal."

Martin and his father, Julian, jumped in the truck they used to haul Mark's race car and drove all night to get home.

"We got home at 6:00 in the morning," Mark remembers. "I took a shower and went to school. Winning that race was the biggest thing that had happened in my life, but at school that Monday, it was like it didn't happen. That's just the way it was."

After Martin graduated from Batesville High, he and his girlfriend, Arlene, decided to tell Arlene's father they were thinking about a wedding.

"Arlene told her dad, 'I'm going to marry this fellow,'" Martin says. "He said, 'What does he do?' Arlene said, 'He's a race car driver.' Her father said, 'No, what does he do for a living?'"

Now, of course, Martin's father-in-law is one of his biggest fans. The fact that Martin has won more than $50 million in the Nextel Cup Series alone has certainly helped that, of course.

Martin started racing when he was just a boy, with his father helping him develop and display his talents. Julian Martin actually started working with Mark long before that. Julian owned a trucking business, and when Mark was barely old enough to stand up in the driver's seat, Julian would let his son steer the truck as Julian controlled the gas and brake pedals.

He'd been racing competitively since 15—he won the third race he ever entered. After every race, Martin would keep a record of how he did and how much money he won. He won a state championship in Arkansas that first year of racing on dirt tracks, and in 1976 moved up to asphalt tracks.

Mark rapidly moved up through the competitive ranks of short-track racing around the Midwest, racing against people sometimes twice or three times his age. He ran against legends like Trickle and Larry Phillips and Larry Shaw. And he did more than hold his own.

Martin won rookie of the year honors in the American Speed Association (ASA) in 1977, then won championships in that series the next three years.

In 1981, Julian and Mark Martin made a foray into NASCAR's top series. Mark, at age 22, made five starts in the Cup Series in 1981—all on short tracks—and never qualified worse than sixth. He won two poles, at Nashville and Richmond, and finished third in his final start that year at Martinsville.

The next season, Martin ran all 30 races and had two top-five finishes, but money promised from sponsors was never delivered. The bills mounted up and, in 1983, he and his father had to auction off their racing equipment to pay them.

Martin eventually returned to the ASA Series for three more seasons, winning another championship in 1986. He tried the

NASCAR Busch Series the following year, driving for car owner
Butch Lawmaster. Martin's win at Dover that year caught the
eye of Jack Roush, a successful sports car racing series owner
looking to make his move into NASCAR.

Roush remembers that when he and Martin talked about
teaming up, Martin didn't ask about how much money he'd be
making or what kind of perks he'd have in his contract. Martin
wanted to know about the cars, about who'd be building them
and working on them. He knew that if his second chance at
NASCAR's top series didn't work out, he'd most likely never get
a third.

But, of course, the Martin-Roush pairing did work out.
Martin got his first Cup win at Rockingham in late 1989, and
he finished third in the championship standings that year.
He'd finish sixth or better in the standings 13 times in the
next 16 seasons and grow to become one of the most
accomplished and respected drivers to ever compete in a
NASCAR race.

Just before the 2005 season began in Daytona, Martin
invited a group of reporters to his office at a private aviation
airport in the Spruce Creek community where he and his family,
which includes budding driver Matt Martin, live.

In that office, Martin had built an impressive trophy case that
was bulging at the seams with all of the hardware he'd won
over the years. He was making plans to get all of those trophies
moved to the new museum in Arkansas.

One trophy in the case stood out.

It was from a win in a Cup race at Watkins Glen. Hanging
from it on small piece of wire was a lug nut with its threads
stripped.

"We should not have won that race," Martin said. "We made a pit stop and put three new tires on; they couldn't change the right rear. We ran that right rear through two stops before we finally got it changed.

"Robin Pemberton, who was changing tires back then wired the nut on there. I walk right up to that and think, 'I remember running two stops and I never dreamed we'd win that race.' But we came back and won. You can look at a lot of those trophies and remember the circumstances involved in winning those races."

That's what the trophies mean to Martin. They're more than just hardware—they represent the stories behind the struggles to succeed.

That's one reason Martin is upset with himself about a decision he made early in his career. He and Arlene were trying to build their lives together, and they wound up moving several times to follow opportunities for Mark to race. Every time they'd move, Mark would pack up the trophies he'd won from the time he was the "oddball" at Batesville High.

One time, finally, Martin decided he wasn't going to move them any more.

"We didn't have a place to put them, and at the time they weren't important to me," Martin said. "Arlene told me it was a bad idea. She said I'd regret it. But I didn't listen."

Years later, Martin saw a trophy that a former rival had kept from a win in an ASA race at the Minnesota state fair. Martin had won that race, too, but he'd discarded the trophy.

"He had that trophy and I looked at that, almost drooling," he said. "I realized, 'Oh my goodness, I don't have one.' I realize now what those meant."

Martin planned to retire from full-time Nextel Cup competition after the 2005 season, but Roush asked him to drive the No. 6 Fords for one more year because he needed him.

After 2006, though, Martin says he's determined to step out of the week-after-week grind of the Cup Series. He plans to race in the NASCAR Craftsman Truck Series and run late models at short tracks wherever he feels like that will be fun.

He'll also keep working on the museum at his dealership in Batesville.

Like a lot of people, whether they're in racing or not, Martin has found that life can be a lot like a race track. Whether you expect to or not, sometimes the finish line winds up being right back where everything started.

"Batesville is place I wanted out of so bad in 1978, I can't tell you," Martin says. "It was way too simple back then for me, but now I long for that simplicity." —D.P.

chapter 13
Wonderboy

Jeff Gordon celebrates after winning Daytona 500, 2-20-05

Rick Hendrick was walking toward the suites on the old frontstretch at Atlanta Motor Speedway—it's the backstretch now—early in the 1992 season. He noticed a car going through the turns smoking its tires because the driver was pushing it so hard.

"Watch that car right there," Hendrick said when he got to where he was going. "He's getting ready to bust his tail."

But the car didn't wreck. It went to victory lane, with Jeff Gordon driving it.

The following Monday, Hendrick was talking about that driver at his team's shop in Charlotte. It just so happened that one of the guys working at the shop was sharing an apartment with Gordon.

By the end of that year, Gordon was driving a Winston Cup car for Hendrick Motorsports. And one of the sport's greatest careers was off and running.

Gordon Goes to School

Jeff Gordon might have been destined to be a stock-car racing star all along, but the path he wound up taking went from California to Indiana to a venerable race track in the sandhills of North Carolina.

The outline of Gordon's pre-NASCAR story is widely known.

At age four, he lived in Vallejo, California, and wanted to race BMX bicycles. His mother, Carol, believed that was too dangerous, but somehow Jeff and his stepfather, John Bickford, convinced his mom that racing a quarter-midget race car would be safer.

By age eight, Gordon had won the national quarter-midget championship. He won it again at age 10 and established himself as a prodigy. In California, though, he couldn't race full-sized sprint cars until he was 18. In Indiana, though, he could move up at age 14.

So Bickford moved his family to Pittsboro, Indiana, and Jeff began racing in the United States Auto Club's (USAC's) national series at all of the tracks in and around Indiana where that kind of racing is done six or seven nights a week in the summer months.

Gordon remembers sitting in class during high school with the guy sitting beside him wearing a Jeff Gordon T-shirt he'd bought at one of those tracks. By 19, Gordon was the USAC national midget series champion. He was also one of the most talked-about young racers in America, thanks to a television show on ESPN called *Thursday Night Thunder*, which carried USAC races to a national cable television audience.

Bickford believed that television could help make his stepson a hot commodity, and he turned out to be exactly right. The Indianapolis-based production company behind *Thursday Night Thunder* came up with the idea to send Gordon to North Carolina Speedway in Rockingham, North Carolina. Buck Baker, the NASCAR legend, had a high-performance driving school that used the track for its classes, and the idea was to turn Jeff Gordon's first trip around a race track in a full-bodied stock car into a feature to air on the *Thursday Night Thunder* show.

What it did, however, was launch a career.

Gordon didn't know what all had been set up for him at Rockingham. Carol had to come with him because Gordon wasn't yet 21 and therefore couldn't rent a car to drive from the airport to the track. "Back in those days, they only told me what I needed to know," Gordon said.

He first went on the track in the school's regular cars. It was set up so the racers in training wouldn't be as likely to spin them around. But it was immediately clear that Gordon was too good for that.

"Buck came over to me after watching me a little bit and said, 'Would you like to get in that Busch car over there?'" Gordon recalled.

The Busch car belonged to Hugh Connerty, who'd been to Baker's school several times. Leo Jackson, who owned Harry Gant's Winston Cup team, was Connerty's father-in-law, and although Connerty was already 41, he still wanted to be a race car driver, too.

Connerty had bought a car Phil Barkdoll had used in Busch Series races. He kept it at Baker's school so that he could come up from his residence in Atlanta and keep trying to improve.

"Buck had called me up and asked me if I'd ever heard of Jeff Gordon," Connerty said. "I said, 'Sure, I've seen him on ESPN.' Buck wanted to know if I would come up and let Jeff drive my car."

So Connerty was there that day to see Gordon's first laps.

"I got in the car and I went pretty good," Gordon said. "We didn't have new tires on it, but I was a lot faster than Hugh was. He came up and said, 'Well, I've learned a lesson today. It's pretty obvious I shouldn't be driving that car.'"

Part of the legend of that day is that Gordon called home to Indiana and told Bickford to sell the sprint cars because he'd found his calling in stock cars.

At the very least, Connerty remembers Gordon's excitement.

"He flew out of the car like he'd won his first race," Connerty said.

Instead of driving the car himself in a few Busch races late in the 1990 season, Connerty put Gordon in the car. Gordon wanted to know who would be working on the car, and Connerty said that Andy Petree, who was Gant's crew chief on the team Connerty's father-in-law owned, had told him about a guy named Ray Evernham

Connerty called Evernham.

"I asked him, 'Have you ever heard of Jeff Gordon?'" Connerty said. "He said, 'Heck, yeah.'"

Connerty arranged for Evernham to come to Lowe's Motor Speedway near Charlotte for a test session. He also had to get Gordon signed, so Jackson gave Connerty a copy of Gant's contract, minus the financial details, as a starting point. So, through Connerty, it was at a test in a Busch car that Evernham and Gordon—the team that would eventually win three Cup championships at Hendrick Motorsports—first met.

Evernham had Chuck Bown shake down the car at the test at Charlotte.

"When Jeff got in it, he took off," Evernham said. "He was flying. He came off one of the bumps in Turn 4 and got real loose in the car. I got on the radio and told him to bring it in. I said, 'Are you all right?' He didn't even know what I was asking him about."

Gordon entered the Charlotte Busch race in a No. 67 Pontiac sponsored by Outback Steakhouse (Connerty ran some restaurants in that franchise). But he wrecked in a qualifying race and didn't make the race.

The next race was at Rockingham. On October 18, 1990, Gordon ran 143.655 mph and qualified on the outside of Row 1 for the ACDelco 200 to be held the next day. He started in front of Dale Earnhardt, Darrell Waltrip, Mark Martin, and Davey Allison. Only Dave Mader, who won the pole at 143.915 mph, went faster.

"We were tight, tight, tight in practice," Evernham said. "We kept saying we needed to loosen the car up. Leo said he didn't think that was a good idea, but we did it anyway."

About 10 laps into the race, Gordon and Evernham understood what Jackson had been saying.

The car was so loose Gordon could barely get it around the track. He was holding on in the top 10, but on lap 34 he crashed on the backstretch. Gordon finished 39th. Steve Grissom won the race, with Earnhardt finishing second.

"After we wrecked," Evernham said, "Leo came up and said, 'The next time you won't worry about being tight, you'll worry about being tight enough.'" —D.P.

A Car Is Declared Extinct

Over the course of NASCAR history, several cars have become infamous for the way they were built to test the edges of the rulebook.

Junior Johnson once built a Ford Galaxy with a chopped off roof and all kinds of twists and turns to its body so that it was nicknamed the "Yellow Banana." NASCAR allowed him to run it because Ford had been out of the sport for a while and the sanctioning body wanted it back in.

In 1987 Bill Elliott won just about every significant race held on the sport's bigger tracks. His No. 9 Ford was widely regarded to be a nearly perfectly "shrunk" version of the rest of the cars on the track—slightly smaller in almost every regard but not too small to fail NASCAR inspection.

One of the most famous cars in the sport's history ran in, and won, the Winston all-star race in 1997. Immediately afterward, NASCAR rewrote several rules to outlaw many of the things that made that car special.

Work on the car began shortly after car owner Rick Hendrick hired engineer Rex Stump in January 1996 and put him in charge of a research and development program for the team.

"It was kind of like our own 'Area 51,'" said Ray Evernham, who was Gordon's crew chief.

About a year later, Stump went to all of the various departments at the Hendrick shop and asked them to try to rethink the whole process of building race cars.

"We said 'If you had a blank sheet of paper, what would you do different in building a race car?'" Stump said. "It was something like 60 different people's ideas on how to make a better car."

Stump had studied what the NASCAR rulebook said—and what it didn't say, too—and figured that there was some wiggle room.

"It seemed we had a little more latitude as to what we could do," Stump said. "So we took it. Any place where there wasn't a rule, we took what we could."

The first time Hendrick saw what his R&D gang was up to, he looked underneath and around the car and said, "There's no way you're going to get to run this car." Hendrick made Stump and his group check in with NASCAR regularly during the car's construction to make sure he was wrong about that.

Generally speaking, the car had bigger frame rails that made the chassis "stiffer" and therefore more resistant to twisting forces as it went around the track. By moving elements in the suspension system as far "outboard" as possible, the car's geometry was also markedly different than existing Cup cars of the day. Every part's weight was carefully considered, as was how that weight was distributed.

As the car's on-track debut approached, it also picked up a nickname. The movie *The Lost World: Jurassic Park*, a sequel to the 1993 hit movie *Jurassic Park*, was about to come out, and the team made a deal to promote it with a special paint scheme. The car got a large dinosaur painted on its hood—a tyrannosaurus rex. Add that to Rex Stump's role in building it, and the car came to be called "T-Rex."

"The valence was pretty high up off the ground," Stump said, speaking of the things trained NASCAR eyes began to notice as soon as the car rolled out at Lowe's Motor Speedway to prepare for the Winston. "You'd walk down and see all the [other cars'] valances 3½ or 4 inches off the ground and this one was 5½ or 6 inches."

While the car sat higher off the ground, the opposite happened when it was going through the turns.

"It was built to 'land' in the middle of the corner to get all of the possible aero benefits, getting it as far down in front as possible and keeping the rear end up," Stump said.

That was a key to what made T-Rex special, Evernham said. "Everything was raised so that when you dropped the nose, it created negative pressure under the car," he said. It was a form of ground effects.

Gordon started 19th after messing up on his pit stop that was part of the qualifying format for the all-star event. But Gordon sliced through the field in the 30-lap first segment of the Winston before settling into third place. Dale Jarrett passed Dale Earnhardt on Lap 25 and won the segment.

Gordon lined up 16th when the field was inverted for the start of segment two. He was fourth, behind Bobby Labonte, Terry Labonte, and Ricky Craven, after those 30 laps, waiting for the right time to show all of his cards.

"I just remember that car being stuck to the track in a way that I had never felt a car be stuck before," he said. "It just gave me confidence, and it was fast—it was awesome."

It took him less than a lap and a half of the final 10-lap segment to take charge. He passed his teammate, Terry Labonte, for the lead and took off.

"When I got by Terry, I said, 'If this thing feels this good for the remainder of this thing, there's no way they can touch me.' We killed them. It was ridiculous."

Gordon had been, perhaps, too strong. His victory, combined with all of the attention the car had been getting before the race from competitors, assured the post-race inspection that night would be vigorous.

"When the race was over, I kind of knew there would be some moaning going on," Hendrick said.

It was more like howling.

"The other car owners looked at it and they all whined and flipped out and said, 'We'll have to build all new cars!'" Evernham said. "Everybody panicked. It's easier to kill Frankenstein than it is to figure out how to get along with him."

Gary Nelson, the man in charge of NASCAR's inspection process at the time, inspected the car before and after the race and said it was legal.

"Every detail of that car had been optimized," Nelson said. "None of it was outside the rules. We looked at the rulebook and there was nothing there that we could use to keep the car from racing. So we said, 'Let's let them race it and get to work on our rulebook.'"

After the race that night, Hendrick and Evernham were told by NASCAR officials that they should not plan on bringing the car back to race again.

"They said, 'Don't bring it back,'" Hendrick said. "I said, 'Hold on a minute. You can't tell me one week that it's okay and then the next week tell me not to bring it back!'"

Evernham also was aghast.

"I said, 'What? Why? It's legal,'" he said. "But they [NASCAR officials] kind of led me to believe that if I did bring it back it wasn't going to get through inspection, and we'd get every kind of pit road penalty you could possibly have."

Hendrick asked NASCAR officials to come to the shop and take a closer look at the car to detail what they didn't like about it. "Maybe that was a mistake, because they spent a good bit of time really looking at the car," Stump said. "Then they went back and wrote a whole bunch of new rules that basically outlawed it."

Stump said at least a half-dozen specific rules were added to NASCAR's rulebook specifically to address issues raised by T-Rex. Nelson won't argue with that estimate.

Ultimately, the Hendrick team realized that if NASCAR wrote rules specific to what it could find in T-Rex, the team might still be able to use the things it hadn't found in its other cars. The team did race T-Rex again—in a state altered to appease NASCAR inspectors—later that year at Indianapolis. The changes hurt the car's performance, and Gordon finished only fourth, but Evernham said the process of building the car that won only once was still worthwhile.

"We learned stuff off of that car that we wound up using inside the new rules they wrote that have helped us on and on and on," Hendrick said. "That car paid big dividends." —D.P.

Getting Gordon's Goat

Jeff Gordon's first career Cup Series start came in the final race of the 1992 season at Atlanta Motor Speedway. Looking back now, it's noteworthy that Gordon's first start came in Richard Petty's last race.

At the drivers' meeting before that race, the Hooters 500, Petty gave each of the drivers who'd qualified for the race a commemorative money clip engraved with the name and date of the race along with the driver's name and his starting position. It also had the words, "Thanks for the Memories, Richard Petty," engraved on it.

Ty Norris, who later went on to work for Earnhardt at Dale Earnhardt Inc., was working for R.J. Reynolds at the time. He was at the drivers' meeting and saw his future boss get into a little mischief.

Gordon, Norris said, was paying rapt attention to the drivers' meeting. Now, the typical drivers' meeting is very much like the safety lecture at the start of an airplane flight. After a while, the passengers could recite it. But this was Gordon's Cup debut, and he didn't want to miss anything.

"He was sitting next to Dale," Norris said. "They're going through all the procedures and Gordon's just focused in on whoever was talking. He was just staring at them, not like a lot of the drivers who are looking around or staring at their watches."

Earnhardt, seeing Gordon so into what was being said at the front of the room, reached off and slipped Gordon's money clip away. Gordon never saw a thing.

"Everybody was finished, and they were walking up to Richard shaking his hand and thanking him," Norris said. "Jeff walked out of the meeting and suddenly remembered he'd forgotten something. He went back to his seat to look for it but it wasn't there. He was running around looking for it.

"Dale was about to fall on the floor laughing. Finally, he walked over to Gordon and said, 'You need to pay attention, kid, this is a pretty big deal.'" —D.P.

A Little Help, Jeff

In 2004, the *Charlotte Observer* allowed me to spend most of the month of June covering different styles of racing off the NASCAR beat. One of the races I attended was the U.S. Grand Prix, a Formula One race at Indianapolis Motor Speedway.

During the week of that race, I was invited to a dinner with some officials of the Toyota F1 team. At this dinner, the conversation inevitably turned to the argument of whether having a competitive American driver in the world's most significant racing series would make F1 more popular in this country, where it has only a loyal but smaller niche following.

As the evening ended, an official with Toyota handed me his business card. "If you come across a good, young American driver who you think could make it in Formula One, you give him this card and have him call me," he said.

I kept the card until I went back onto the NASCAR beat for the July 4 weekend race at Daytona International Speedway. On the first day of practice, I asked Jon Edwards, Gordon's outstanding public relations man, to get me five minutes with Gordon. And I told Jon he needed to be there, too.

After a practice session, I walked up into the back of the No. 24 team's hauler with Gordon and Edwards. Both are big F1 fans, so it wasn't any problem getting that topic brought up.

I told Gordon about the dinner with the Toyota folks. I told him about the business card and I pulled it out my pocket.

You have to realize that about twice each year since Gordon has been a NASCAR star, somebody has started a rumor saying that he might leave stock-car racing to go drive an F1 car. He actually tested one at Indy, in a PR stunt for the track in which he and Juan Pablo Montoya "switched" cars for a few laps.

"Jeff," I said, "this gentleman told me to get this card to an outstanding young American driver who might have a future in F1."

Gordon smiled.

And then, I got my punch line out.

"Could you please give this card to Jimmie Johnson for me?" I asked.

Edwards nearly fell in the floor laughing.—D.P.

chapter 14
Young Guns

*Carl Edwards does backflip after winning
the NASCAR Busch Aaron's 312, 3-19-05*

Jeff Gordon's success in NASCAR convinced a lot of people that young drivers could get the job done, and get it done well. Gordon won 55 races before his 30th birthday. Only Richard Petty, with 60, won more before turning 30.

In the years since Gordon's arrival, these young drivers have begun to make their own mark on the sport. None of them has quite matched Gordon's early career pace, but they've done all right for themselves.

That Carl Edwards—He's a Card

It's not exactly "Will Work for Food," but it's close.

Carl Edwards exploded onto the Nextel Cup racing scene in 2005, earning his first victory in NASCAR's top series at Atlanta Motor Speedway in just the fourth race of his first full season as driver of the No. 99 Fords owned by Jack Roush.

He passed Jimmie Johnson off the final turn on the final lap to get that victory, just one day after he'd earned his first career victory in the Busch Series at the same track.

After both wins, Edwards did back flips off the window sill of his race car. The celebration was something he saw an open-wheel driver do once, and Edwards thought it was cool. So he copied the move when he started winning races in NASCAR's Truck Series. Now, it has become his trademark.

Edwards is unique, there's no question about that. He came into stock-car racing's top series with a wide-eyed exuberance that quickly endeared him to NASCAR fans.

The story of how Edwards got to Nextel Cup is unique, too.

His father, Carl "Mike" Edwards, owned a Volkswagen repair shop and won more than 200 features in various forms of racing around the Midwest. Carl Jr. followed in those footsteps, beginning his career in four-cylinder VWs at the age of 14.

Edwards' father is a cousin of NASCAR driver Ken Schrader, and when Carl Jr. was 17, he went to work in Schrader's shop.

"That kind of turned racing into a reality for me," Edwards says. "I was mowing the grass at the shop and going to the races and helping out, and I realized these guys were all just guys who go racing at home every week, just at a different level.

I went home and decided it was time to get going, to learn how to race."

He drove dirt-track modifieds and won track championships at Capital Speedway in Holt Summit, Missouri, in 1999 and 2000, then moved on to the U.S. Auto Club's Silver Crown Series.

All the while, Edwards was looking for a way to get his foot into the door in NASCAR. He had a friend who was an aspiring actor, and that friend had a card with his photograph and biographical information on it that he could hand out at auditions.

"So I thought, 'Man, I need to get a card or some sort of piece of information that I can give to people,'" Edwards said. "I sat down and talked to my mom [Nancy Sterling] about it, and she said, 'You need a business card. You need a business card that says you want to drive race cars.' And I thought, 'Man, that's great.'"

Edwards went to a print shop in his hometown of Columbia, Missouri.

"They gave me a great deal," he said. "It was like $100 for 2,000 business cards with my picture on them and everything on it. My whole resume was on the back—not in very small print either—but I had a resume and I just started handing them out to everyone. I think I passed out 2,500 of them.

"Everywhere I went I always had business cards. I figured eventually the whole world would know that I wanted to drive race cars and there would be some owner that would need a driver and somebody would say, 'Man, you ought to hire him.'"

After Edwards arrived on the Nextel Cup scene, fellow driver Tony Stewart talked about seeing the card that Edwards had printed in the classified ads section of *National Speed*

Sport News, laughing at the idea that anybody thought that might work.

But in 2002, Edwards got his shot. He made seven starts for a Truck Series team owned by Mike Mittler, getting only one top-10 finish.

But he did well enough with a team that was fighting uphill financially to get noticed by some of the folks at Roush Racing, who were about to unexpectedly need a Truck Series driver for the 2003 season.

Roush planned to put Kyle Busch in a truck that season once Busch reached his 18th birthday in May. But before the season started, Busch signed to drive at Hendrick Motorsports, leaving Roush with a team but no driver.

So a door opened for Edwards, and he walked through it. Edwards won three races and took rookie of the year honors. Edwards won three more Truck races in 2004, and when Jeff Burton left the No. 99 team to jump to Richard Childress Racing, Roush put Edwards into that car.

"Everything just worked out perfectly," Edwards said. "I had a lot of really good people. My mom and her husband, Jim Sterling, are unbelievable. They've helped me so much. My mom has always been my backbone and supported me so much. My dad is the smartest racer in the world, and I feel like the things I do on the race track and the way that I approach racing is because of my father."

After the victory at Atlanta, Edwards surprised his mother by buying her a new car.

Life, in other words, is good.

"Just look at what we're doing," Edwards said. "It's the neatest thing in the world....We get to go out there and drive as hard as we can and think as hard as we can about how to make the cars faster. You're competing against other human beings, which is the neatest thing in the world. We get to go out there and risk it all and race for glory and all that. It's the most fun thing in the world. It's just awesome. I mean, this is as good as it gets. It's unbelievable, and I'm enjoying every minute of it." —D.P.

Working for a Living

Sometimes, people actually do have a "Eurkea!" moment.

It's an instant when the picture becomes clear and they understand where they want to go with their lives. It happened, for instance, to Nextel Cup championship-winning driver Tony Stewart.

"I was working at a machine shop for $5 an hour in the middle of the country in Rush County, Indiana," Stewart said. "I sat in a big barn on a metal stool on a concrete floor at a drill press and was picking up parts out of a 5-gallon bucket full of solvent.

"It was a good thing I actually started the job before winter came because I knew the roads good enough. You had to blow through the snow drifts just to get to and from work."

Stewart was also driving race cars. He had been ever since he was a boy growing up in Columbus, Indiana, where he'd convinced the owner of the local Dairy Queen to sponsor his go-karts by letting him have free chocolate milk shakes. Stewart was racing midgets and sprint cars by the time he had the job in the machine shop, and he was good, too.

That winter, he took a USAC Silver Crown division car to the Copper World Classic in Phoenix and finished second to Mike Bliss.

"My portion of the prize money was, like, $3,500," Stewart said. "When I came back to work on Monday, I was sitting at that drill press and started trying to figure out how many $5 hours I had to work to make $3,500.

"I thought, 'When I drive race cars I can get up at noon. I'm at the pit gate by 4:00. I'm done at midnight, and I'm still wide awake. If I can do that three nights a week and pay my bills I don't have to get up at 7:30 and drive to work and work five days a week."

Eureka! —D.P.

Gone, but Not Forgotten

About six weeks before the 2001 NASCAR season began, Dale Earnhardt Jr. sat in front of the media and talked about a dream he'd had.

He dreamed about the 2001 Daytona 500—and about winning it. "I was out front all day," he said of the dream. "I kept telling myself I won it in my second time in the race."

His father had won the 500 in 1998 and was the acclaimed master of racing on NASCAR's restrictor-plate tracks.

Somebody asked Earnhardt Jr. where Dale Earnhardt's black No. 3 Chevrolet was in the dream.

"Dad," Earnhardt Jr. said, "wasn't there."

Those words took on an eerie feel on February 19.

On the final lap of the Daytona 500, Earnhardt Jr. wasn't exactly out front. He was second, running behind new teammate Michael Waltrip.

Earnhardt was there, running third right behind the two cars his Dale Earnhardt Inc. team owned.

But then, he was gone.

The images flash in the memories of race fans everywhere.

A crash in Turn 4. Earnhardt's car snapping up the track and running into the outside wall with frightening force. Ken Schrader jumping out of his car, which had rammed into the side of the black No. 3 an instant before it nosed into the wall, and running to check on his friend and rival. An ambulance carrying Earnhardt leaving the track slowly, much too slowly.

And then, the awful news.

Dale Earnhardt, who had for so long seemed so indestructible, had been killed.

It didn't seem possible. As difficult as it was for the fans to believe, imagine how hard his father's death was for Earnhardt Jr. to understand. Of all the things Earnhardt Jr. ever wanted to achieve in a race car, earning his father's respect was right at the top of that list.

"It's like a never-ending process," Earnhardt Jr. said of his efforts to do that. "It's bottomless. I get worn out by it at times. But it's something you always want. Sometimes it becomes more important than the job at hand. What other reason do you race for? You race for thousands of dollars. That's good. You race to win. That's good. Those are good reasons. But there's nothing wrong with wanting to make my dad happy."

And then, he was gone.

"I thought he was Superman," Earnhardt Jr. said.

Five months later, Earnhardt Jr. had to come back to Daytona to race again. The Pepsi 400 in July would be one of the most emotional races of his young life, no matter how well he ran. And when Earnhardt Jr. won the race, it was one of the most emotional moments the sport has ever known.

Earnhardt Jr. had come to Daytona a couple of days early that summer. He went down in Turn 4, near the spot where his father had crashed. He sat there, thinking about all he'd seen his father do and all he'd learned from watching it. And he made a kind of peace with Daytona. His dad had loved racing there. Earnhardt had cherished all of his many successes at Daytona, and he absolutely reveled in his victory in the Daytona 500 in 1998 that had ended a career filled with frustration.

"In a way, it feels like I'm closer to Dad when [I'm] here," Earnhardt Jr. said of Daytona. "But at the same time, you get reminded of losing him all over again."

Earnhardt Jr. had begun to show prowess on restrictor-place tracks that reminded everyone of his father, but, like his dad, he'd missed out on a couple of potential opportunities to win the Daytona 500.

"There are days when I feel like I am as good as he was," Earnhardt Jr. said. "But then you're reminded by something that reminds you of what he did that you'll never be able to do. There are times on the track where I get real confident and feel like I couldn't have done it any better than that right there. But it's not long before I figure out I'm wrong.

"He was pretty tough. You have to watch some old tape to see things he did on the track to remind you how slick he was and how determined he was. He always figured it out, you know?"

But in February 2004, Earnhardt Jr. got a victory in NASCAR's biggest race. It was a memorable day, beginning with President George W. Bush flying in on Air Force One before the race to participate in the ceremonies before the start of another season. The president actually called the start of the race in the Motor Racing Network's radio booth, with long-time play-by-play announcer Barney Hall giving an assist.

After the race, as he stood in the press box doing his post-race interviews, someone handed Earnhardt Jr. a cell phone. The president, who'd left during the race, was calling to say congratulations.

It had taken his father 20 tries to win the Daytona 500. Earnhardt Jr. did it in his fifth.

"He was over in the passenger seat riding with me," Earnhardt Jr. said of his late father. "I'm sure he was having a blast."

That wasn't the last time Earnhardt Jr. felt his father's presence around him in a race car. In July 2004, during a weekend off on the Nextel Cup schedule, Earnhardt Jr. went to the Infineon Raceway road course to compete in an American Le Mans Series race with a factory-backed Chevrolet team. In a warm-up session on the morning of the race, Earnhardt Jr. crashed, and the car erupted in flames.

Somehow, Earnhardt Jr. managed to unbuckle himself and escape the inferno. He suffered burns that forced him to get out of the car early in subsequent Cup races, but he survived.

When he got to the hospital on that day, Earnhardt Jr. grabbed DEI team official Steve Crisp, who'd gone with him to California for that race, and told Crisp that he had to find "the guy who pulled me out of the car."

Crisp told Earnhardt Jr. that nobody had pulled him out.

At first, Earnhardt Jr. didn't say much about what had happened—and about what he thought had happened. But several months later, he recalled what he felt while he was in that fire.

"I reached up into the roll bar to pull myself out, somebody grabbed me underneath the arms, I thought, and pulled me out of the car," Earnhardt Jr. said. "It was as real as [it could be]. It was no dream or whatever. Call me crazy; I don't care. That was an experience that only I know and only I can tell it.

"I swear somebody had me underneath my arms and was carrying me out of the car," Earnhardt Jr. said. "I mean, I swear to God."

Earnhardt Jr. told that story for the first time in an interview on *60 Minutes* with famed journalist Mike Wallace.

"And that was your dad?" Wallace asked.

"I don't know," Earnhardt Jr. said. "You tell me. It freaks me just talking about it. It just gives me chills." —D.P.

.

sources

Chapin, Kim. *Fast as White Lightning*. New York: Dial Press, 1981.

Cutter, Robert and Fendell, Bob. *Encyclopedia of Auto Racing Greats*. Englewood Cliffs, NJ: Prentice-Hall, 1973.

Engel, Lyle Kenyon. *Stock Car Racing USA*. New York: Dodd, Mead and Co., 1973.

Fielden, Greg. *High Speed at Low Tide*. Surfside Beach, SC: Galfied Press, 1993.

Fielden, Greg. *Forty Years of Stock Car Racing: Vol. I, The Beginning 1949–1958*. Pinehurst, NC: Garfield Press, 1988.

Fielden, Greg. *Forty Years of Stock Car Racing: Vol. II, The Speedway Boom, 1959–1964*. Pinehurst, NC: Garfield Press, 1988.

Fielden, Greg. *Forty Years of Stock Car Racing: Vol. III, Big Bucks and Boycotts, 1965–1971*. Pinehurst, NC: Garfield Press, 1988.

Fielden, Greg. *Forty Years of Stock Car Racing: Vol. IV, The Modern Era, 1972–1989*. Pinehurst, NC: Garfield Press, 1988.

Fielden, Greg. *Rumblin' Ragtops: The History of NASCAR's Fabulous Convertible Division*. Pinehurst, NC: Garfield Press, 1990.

Golenbock, Peter. *American Zoom: Stock Car Racing–From the Dirt Tracks to Daytona*. New York: McMillan Publishing Co., 1993.

Higgins, Tom. *That's Racin'.com, Tom Higgins' Scuffs.* Knight Ridder Digital, Sept. 15, 2005.

Higgins, Tom and Waid, Steve. *Junior Johnson, Brave in Life.* Phoenix, AZ: David Bull Publishing, 1999.

Hunter, Jim. *Darlington Raceway 50th Anniversary.* Charlotte, NC: UMI Publications, 1999.

McLaurin, Jim. *NASCAR's Most Wanted: The Top 10 Book of Outrageous Drivers, Wild Wrecks, and Other Oddities.* Washington, D.C.: Brassey's, 2001.

Yarborough, Cale and Neely, William. *Cale: The Hazardous Life and Times of the World's Greatest Stock Car Driver.* New York: Times Books, 1986.

Yunick, Smokey. *All Right You Sons-a-Bitches, Let's Have a Race!* Daytona Beach, FL: Carbon Press, 2001.

HICKMANS

7/05